INSTITUTE OF HUMAN RELATIONS : YALE UNIVERSITY

ESSENTIALS OF BEHAVIOR

ESSENTIALS OF BEHAVIOR

by Clark L. Hull

GREENWOOD PRESS, PUBLISHERS
WESTPORT, CONNECTICUT

Library of Congress Cataloging in Publication Data

Hull, Clark Leonard, 1884-1952.
 Essentials of behavior.

 Reprint of the 1951 ed. published by Yale
University Press, New Haven, Conn.
 Bibliography: p.
 1. Conditioned response. I. Title.
[BF319.H83 1974]   152.3'2   73-8150
 ISBN 0-8371-6956-9

Originally published in 1951 for The Institute of Human
Relations by Yale University Press, New Haven

Reprinted with the permission of Yale University Press

Reprinted from an original copy in the collections of the
University of Illinois Library

Reprinted by Greenwood Press, Inc.

First Greenwood reprinting 1973
Second Greenwood reprinting 1977

Library of Congress catalog card number 73-8150
ISBN 0-8371-6956-9

Printed in the United States of America

Preface

THIS VOLUME is designed to present briefly and in an intelligible manner the basic laws of mammalian behavior, and to serve as a useful introduction to the current aspects of behavior theory. During the last eight years the fundamental hypotheses of my system have matured considerably. This development will be reflected in the system itself, which I hope to publish within a year or two.

I must take this occasion to express my indebtedness to Frederick S. Cates, Jr., who made the drawings for nearly all of the figures appearing in this work. John A. Antoinetti and Harry G. Yamaguchi performed most of the mathematical and equation-fitting operations which are used; in addition, Mr. Antoinetti prepared the glossary of symbols and the subject index, and Dr. Yamaguchi has kindly permitted the presentation here of certain material contained in his doctoral dissertation. I must thank Ruth Hays for her indispensable aid in the preparation of the manuscript. Finally, I wish to express my indebtedness to the Institute of Human Relations, to Professor Mark A. May, its Director, and to Yale University for the opportunity to perform the task.

C. L. H.

New Haven
March, 1951

Contents

1. Introduction

IN THE FOLLOWING PAGES are presented, with appropriate explanations, what are regarded at the present time as the basic or primary laws (postulates) of mammalian behavior. There are also given a few secondary, i.e., derived, laws (corollaries) which we believe will more frequently be used in deducing the system than will the ordinary theorem.

The primary laws of the present behavior system are all empirical in nature; i.e., they have all originated in one way or another from observation and experiment. Yet all these primary principles are here called postulates. This superficial paradox arises in part because it is always more or less of an assumption to hold that any experiment reveals the true law which is sought; to present an empirical generalization as a *primary* law, as distinguished from a secondary or derived law, is still more of an assumption.

During the years since the publication of *Principles of Behavior*, numerous reasons for changes and modifications in the postulates as there presented have been revealed.

These have arisen through a careful study of experimental results from Yale laboratories and from laboratories in other institutions, numerous thoughtful theoretical criticisms, and our use of the postulates of the system in making concrete deductions of the systematic details of individual (non-social) behavior. As a consequence the mathematical aspects of many of the postulates have been formulated, or reformulated, and the verbal formulation of nearly all has been modified to a certain extent. One postulate (*30*, p. 319) has been dropped in part as empirically erroneous; some postulates have been divided and others have been combined; several new postulates have been added; and a number of the original postulates have been deduced from others of the present set and appear as corollaries in these pages.

Psychology as a systematic science is relatively young. As a consequence it is to be expected that as time goes on marked changes will continue to be made in the fundamental assumptions underlying the systematizations. The fearless performance of critical experiments and the continuous quantitative use of the relevant postulates and corollaries will hasten the elimination of errors and the day when mammalian behavior will take its place among the recognized quantitative systematic sciences. This work has been prepared as a contribution to that end.

2. Unlearned Stimulus-Response Connections ($_sU_R$)

WHEN VERTEBRATES first enter the external world they are possessed of certain tendencies to respond to stimuli or stimulus combinations, especially to stimuli which are associated with biological emergencies called needs. As a rule these unlearned acts tend to reduce or totally abolish the need in question. Owing to the complexity and variety of conditions under which the needs of most animals arise, an act which will reduce a need in one situation will not do it so effectively, or at all, in another. This problem in biological survival is met by the fact that most unlearned responses to a need, if long enough continued, become very variable both in nature and intensity. If the first response does not bring a reduction or abolition of the need, a later one may do so. Thus biological survival is favored by a kind of primitive trial and error.

Generalizing from the preceding and related considerations, we arrive at our first primary molar behavior principle or postulate (*30*, p. 66):

I. Organisms at birth possess receptor-effector connections ($_SU_R$) which under combined stimulation (S) and drive (D) have the potentiality of evoking a hierarchy of responses that either individually or in combination are more likely to terminate the need than would be a random selection from the reactions resulting from the other stimulus and drive combinations.

3. Behavior Theory versus Neurophysiology

USUALLY ORGANISMS must act to reduce needs. In order that the activity may be effective in this, the responses must ordinarily be adapted to the nature, intensity, and temporal onset of the need, often very precisely. This means that the need and its associated circumstances must somehow be brought to bear on the acting or effector organs of the animal. This is achieved through the mediation of the various receptors or sense organs which are capable of being differentially stimulated by the various energies involved in the several possible needs and associated stimulating conditions.

When a need stimulates a receptor the resulting afferent neural impulse proceeds toward the central ganglia which act as a kind of automatic "switchboard," directing the impulse to the muscles or glands whose action is necessary to reduce the particular need. Unfortunately, the knowledge of neurophysiology has not yet advanced to a point where it is of much assistance in telling us how the nervous system operates in the determination of important forms of behavior. This means that our theory of behavior must be at bottom almost entirely molar; i.e., it must be presented in terms of stimuli and responses together with a statement of the conditions under which these have occurred in the past and are about to occur in the present.

Now while this molar or non-neurophysiological approach presumably permits a much less perfect behavioral science than will someday be possible with a full knowledge of neurophysiology, it does give us a great deal of understanding of behavior. True, we occasionally mention certain aspects of the presumably associated neural activities of behavior in order to remind our readers that the ultimate physical action determining behavior does not occur in a vacuum, that it is essentially neural, even though that fact helps us at present hardly at all in the detailed deduction of adaptive behavior.

The test of the soundness of the present theory is the agreement of our equations with the quantitative observations of the antecedent conditions in relation to the sequent behavior. Specifically, in presenting the postulate regarding stimulus reception (S and s, Postulate II), we do not propose to delve into neurophysiology in order to test its molar soundness; we intend only, when interpreting the results of quantitative stimulation (which must evidently involve s as well as S), to do so in terms of log S rather than merely S. The same holds in regard to the postulate concerning afferent interaction (š, Postulate XII), and indeed all of the symbolic constructs such as $_sH_R$, $_sE_R$, and so on. Meanwhile in case these postulates stand up under logical utilization, they may serve as a suggestive lead to neurophysiologists in their empirical investigations, and ultimately to a higher integration of gross molar behavior and neurophysiology.

4. The Molar Stimulus Trace (s') and Its Stimulus Equivalent (S')

LET US REPRESENT the intensity of any physical stimulus energy by S. Analogically, we shall represent by s the neurophysiological intensity of the functioning afferent impulse propagated toward the effectors. There is reason to believe that during the action of S on the receptor sensitive to it the intensity of s rises from zero very rapidly to a maximum after which it gradually falls to an unspecified level (*30*, p. 42) even though S continues its action. However, there is also reason to believe that s may not directly become reinforced to responses, but does so indirectly through some additional molar process of unknown physiological nature. The main evidence for this is that the submolar impulse (s) from the receptor seems to reach its maximum sooner than the corresponding molar impulse (s') appears to do so. Our knowledge of this molar afferent impulse is essentially indirect. This naturally produces great difficulty in our determination of its quantitative characteristics, and at the same time lays us open to special danger of making errors in so doing. Nevertheless the importance of the matter in the dynamics of behavior is so great that this risk must be taken.

Since it will be more convenient to deal with the intensities of these molar afferent impulses in the form of their *equivalent functional* stimulus intensities, we shall do so, representing the latter by the symbol S'. For analogous reasons we shall represent the molar trace itself by s'. Much evidence indicates that molar stimulus traces, like their neurophysiological correlates (s), have a brief *recruitment phase* ($\dot{S}'$, $\dot{s}'$) which is followed by a relatively protracted falling or *subsident phase* ($\underset{.}{S}'$, $\underset{.}{s}'$). These two phases of the molar afferent impulse or trace are indicated in a significant manner by some experimental conditioning results found by Reynolds (*61*) and by Kimble (*41*).

Reynolds conditioned an eyelid blink reaction, originally produced by an airpuff on the cornea, to the after-effects of a single auditory click lasting only .050″, at four different ages of the trace: .250″, .450″, 1.15″, and 2.25″. Kimble's results were secured by his conditioning the airpuff blink to a continuous visual stimulus at various intervals after its onset: .100″, .200″, .222″, .250″, .300″, and .400″. (So far as the empirical data available at present go, there does not appear to be much difference between the molar after-effects of a continuous stimulus and those of a very brief stimulus.) It is quite clear from the results of these studies as well as from those of earlier experiments (e.g., *76; 77*) that responses conditioned to stimulus after-effects of various ages result in reaction potentials of characteristic $_sE_R$ intensities. These are represented graphically in Figure

1. As a matter of fact, these gradients indicate theoretically a corresponding change in s'.

From the calculated reaction potentials shown in Figure 1 we have, by a procedure to be explained in a

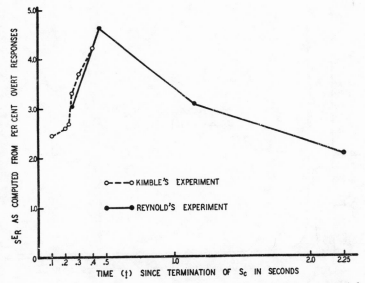

Figure 1. Graphic representation of empirical reaction-potential results reported by Reynolds (61) and Kimble (41), from which were calculated the recruitment and the subsident gradients shown in somewhat idealized form in Figure 2. The time indication in the figure holds only for Reynolds' results, since the Kimble times were continuous from the beginning.

forthcoming work, secured a first approximation to the equivalent stimulus intensities (S'). An equation was fitted to the recruitment phase of the S' values calculated from the Kimble data, and another one to the subsident phase of the S' values calculated from the

Reynolds data. It turns out that both fitted equations are probably power functions. Adapting some irregularities in the empirical results presumably due mainly to the sampling limitations of the original data or to

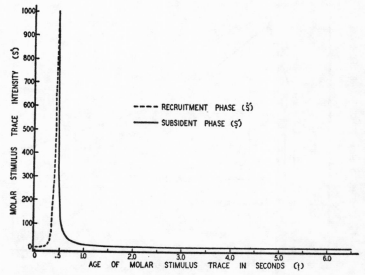

Figure 2. Graphic representation of the two phases of the postulated equivalent stimulus intensity (S') of the molar stimulus trace (s') following the presentation of a brief stimulus. The stimulus intensity is taken at a conventional maximum of 1,000 units, though this will vary with the sense involved and the unit employed.

artifacts such as spontaneous winks and so on, we have the two equations represented by the two curves of Figure 2. These are the bases for parts A and B of our next postulate.

Generalizing on the preceding considerations, we arrive at our second postulate (*30*, p. 43):

II. A. When a brief stimulus (S) impinges upon a suitable receptor there is initiated the recruitment phase of a self-propagating molar afferent trace impulse (ṡ'), the molar stimulus equivalent (S') of which rises as a power function of time (ṭ) since the beginning of the stimulus, i.e.,

$$\dot{S}' = 465{,}190 \times \underset{.}{t}^{7.6936} + 1.0, \tag{1}$$

$\dot{S}'$ reaching its maximum (and termination) when $\underset{.}{t}$ equals about .450″.

B. Following the maximum of the recruitment phase of the molar stimulus trace, there supervenes a more lengthy subsident phase (ṣ'), the stimulus equivalent of which descends as a power function of time (ṭ'), i.e.,

$$\underset{.}{S}' = 6.9310(\underset{.}{t}' + .01)^{-1.0796}, \tag{2}$$

where $\underset{.}{t}' = \underset{.}{t} - .450″$.

C. The intensity of the molar stimulus trace (s') is a logarithmic function of the molar stimulus equivalent of the trace, i.e.,

$$s' = \log S'. \tag{3}$$

5. Reaction Potential ($_sE_R$) and Its Quantification

WHENEVER A STIMULUS impinges on the normal stimulus receptors of an organism there is the potentiality of a reaction. This may be the potentiality of an innate or unlearned reaction or of a learned reaction. It may lead to an overt reaction or it may be so weak or so much opposed by other reaction potentialities existent at the same time that it produces no observable reaction whatever. This means that the potentiality of an act ($_sE_R$) is not an act or a movement or anything which can be directly observed. Instead, it is a quantitative theoretical construct. No doubt the physical reality directly behind this construct lies in the nervous system, much as in the case of s and š considered above, and, as with them, this presumptive neural substratum is at present directly inaccessible to us.

This means that an indirect molar method must be employed in the quantification of reaction potential. The basis for such a quantificational method exists in Thurstone's Case III adaptation (69; 70; 71) of the psychophysical method of paired comparisons, as originally developed in connection with the empirical investigations relating to the Weber-Fechner law. Thurstone's procedure is based on the subject's judgments of greater or less, and the unit of quantification at bottom rests on the mean variability in the subject's judgments of the several items involved. Moreover, the things being compared are in some sense present to the subject when the comparison is being made.

In the methodology for the quantification of reaction potential, on the other hand, the subject makes no comparisons. He merely produces concrete reactions which must possess some objectively measurable monotonic indication of the intensity of the tendency to perform the act. An obvious case of such an indication is seen in the intensity of struggling movements (in grams), or the amount of salivary secretion (in cubic centimeters) produced by hungry organisms when presented with not-quite accessible food. Other things equal, the more intense the movement or the more saliva secreted, the greater will be the associated $_sE_R$. A dozen or so of such indirect monotonic indicators of the degree of reaction potentiality have been identified (*39*, p. 238). The only indicator which has actually been used in this way, so far, is reaction latency ($_st_R$); other things equal, the shorter the latency the greater is the associated $_sE_R$.

The procedure with which we are here concerned is a special form of quantification by means of a *scale* (*71; 39*). The natural unit to be used in such cases is the standard deviation (*17*) of the variability of the phenomenon under investigation—in this case, $_sE_R$. At bottom this is based on the variability, or inconsistency, of the responses which serve as the basis for the quantification. The inconsistency in the case of judgments is shown by the subject's sometimes judging the first of a comparison pair as the greater, and sometimes the second. Ultimately the degree of the difference between the two is derived from the per cent of comparisons in which one compared object is considered greater than the other. In the $_sE_R$ quantification technique the comparisons are made by the investigator presumably without error. The inconsistency or variability is shown, for example, by the first compared response sometimes having a shorter latency than the second, and the second sometimes having a shorter latency than the first. The difference in reaction potential is derived from the per cent of a large number of such comparisons in which the one reaction latency is shorter than the other.

As yet this $_sE_R$ quantificational procedure is fairly new and much remains to be determined. However, several fairly elaborate studies have been made (*39; 79; 74*), and their results will be cited from time to time. The present outline of the procedure is given as a specific introduction to the central quantitative concept of the theoretical system. And finally, the procedure of the quantification may be regarded as an operational definition of $_sE_R$.

6. Primary Motivation and Reinforcement

ORGANISMS REQUIRE on the whole a rather precise set of conditions for optimal chances of individual and species survival. When these conditions deviate appreciably from the optimum a state of need is said to exist, and a more or less persistent stimulation (S_D) arises. This drive state (S_D) evokes some of the hierarchy of unlearned impulses ($_sU_R$). In case none of these responses diminishes the need, the organism may die or fail to reproduce. With some species, especially early in life, death occurs on a large scale. If, however, any of the evoked movements chances to reduce the receptor discharge characteristic of a need (S_D), the stimuli and the stimulus traces operating on the organism's sensorium at the time acquire an increment of connection of such a nature that on subsequent occasions if any of these stimuli recurs in conjunction with the drive the reaction will tend to be evoked. We shall call this the *law of reinforcement*.

There are two types of learning situations which appear superficially to be fairly different from each other and which, in fact, have been considered by some as being essentially distinct. These are (1) simple associative or elementary trial-and-error learning, and (2) conditioned-reflex learning. The evidence regarding the problem is not complete as yet, so that an absolute decision cannot be made. Nevertheless we are of the opinion that simple associative learning and conditioned-reflex learning are essentially identical in that they are based on the same major principle—the law of reinforcement (*30*, pp. 68–80); that the difference between the two consists only in the circumstances under which the major principle operates. In the typical simple associative or elementary trial-and-error situation the conditions evoke numerous alternative reactions, e.g., corner sniffing as shown in Figure 3 ($S_2 \rightsquigarrow R_1$). But the reaction which promptly brings forth the reinforcement (e.g., bar pressing) has a weaker potentiality than some of the others and is not the first to occur. However, when the bar-pressing reaction is finally evoked, reinforcement occurs at once and an increment of strength is added to the reaction potential ($S_2 \dashrightarrow R_2$) which originally evoked it. This is represented by the broken-line connection from the apparatus stimulus to the bar-pressing reaction in addition to the wavy causal connection already existent. Moreover, any other stimuli which may be present, e.g., the buzzer vibration (S_1), will acquire *de novo* an increment of a connection ($S_1 \dashrightarrow R_2$) for this stimulus also to evoke this response on a subsequent occasion as shown by the broken-line connection unaccompanied by the wavy line. Thus we have here two distinguishable forms of learning, (1) the strengthening of an earlier bond, and (2) the establishment of a new

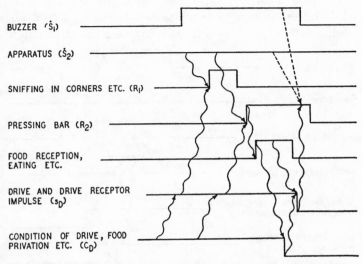

Figure 3. Diagram representing the origin of the simple associative or trial-and-error learning process by which the bar-pressing habit is established. First the drive condition (C_D) causes the s_D which, combined with the apparatus stimulation, causes sniffing in the corners, reaching up on the sides of the cage, and so on (R_1), but no reinforcement results from these acts. However, when the drive and apparatus stimulation subsequently produce an act which depresses the bar, a pellet of food is delivered. The eating of the food reduces the drive condition and this reduces the drive stimulus. It is believed that the reduction in s_D is the critical factor in the reinforcement and provides the condition for the setting up of the S $\dashrightarrow$ R connection by which $\dot{S}_1$ and S_2 later jointly evoke the bar-pressing response rather than that of sniffing. The broken lines represent acquired receptor-effector connections, and the wavy lines represent ordinary causal connections.

one. Both types of acquisition, particularly the strengthening of a bond already in existence, are typical of the trial-and-error type of learning. As repetitions continue both of these two bonds will increase in strength as

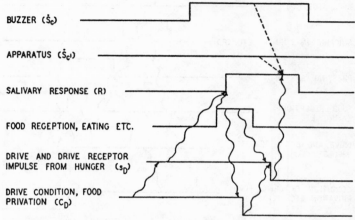

Figure 4. Diagram representing the origin of the Pavlovian conditioned salivary reflex. The food privation or drive condition (C_D) causes the drive (D) and the drive stimulus (s_D). The drive stimulus combined with the eating of food initially evokes the salivary response. The food reception also eventually causes a diminution in the drive condition and in the s_D. This latter is believed to constitute the reinforcing agent which produces the S --→ R bonds connecting the buzzer and the apparatus as stimuli with the response. The broken lines represent acquired receptor-effector connections, and the wavy lines represent ordinary causal connections.

compared with the initially stronger bonds ($S_2 \leadsto R_1$), such as sniffing, etc., until they finally become dominant. At this point learning would ordinarily be said to be complete, though in fact it is not.

On the other hand, the bond acquired *de novo*, as shown in Figure 3, is essential to conditioned-reflex learning as represented in Figure 4. But in the condi-tioned-reflex type of learning, while presumably there is a hierarchy of other unlearned reaction potentials evoked by the initial stimulus situation, the member of the hierarchy which will be reinforced is the dominant one, i.e., *the first and only obvious response to occur*. Moreover, there is ordinarily provided in conditioned-reflex experi-ments an initially neutral stimulus to receive the *de novo* reinforcement connection to the dominant response. In the course of subsequent trials the connection between S_c and R grows strong enough so that S will evoke R *before* the food reinforcement is given, at which time the conditioned reflex is ordinarily said to have been estab-lished, though it would not have attained its maximum strength.

The two examples of reinforcement given above have emphasized the learning of fairly simple and specific acts. Now it must be added that often the stimuli in-volved in reinforcement may concern fairly complex percepts themselves, based on previously formed habits such as visual perceptions of distance; and the responses may also be based on well-worn habits such as locomo-tion and leaping. It is the *connection* of the stimuli to the responses which is new and results from the reinforce-ment. Consider a cat learning to pursue a mouse. The cat's eyes converge on the mouse. The degree of binocular convergence, coupled with the size of the retinal images, etc., in previously reinforced situations involving short distances, furnishes excellent bases for the stealthy loco-motor approach—the running and the leaping involved in the pursuit. This type of learning, while involving complexities on both the stimulus and response sides, requires relatively little new learning because most of the complexities on both sides were already integrated incidentally to reinforcement in other situations before the present reinforcement began. This type of economy has been suggested experimentally.

But if the mouse should always be found in the same place, the cat would always go to that place for food, especially if he could see the mouse at a distance, regardless of what differences of locomotor movements are involved. The point is that locomotion is largely guided in such situations by optical fixation. In this way, it is believed, the learning of location or place comes about. Thus place-learning and act-learning are believed to be essentially alike in their reinforcement rather than distinct, as has sometimes been supposed.

Generalizing on the preceding considerations, we arrive at the following postulate (30, p. 80):

> III. Whenever an effector activity (R) is closely associated with a stimulus afferent impulse or trace (s) and the conjunction is closely associated with the rapid diminution in the motivational stimulus (S_D or s_G), there will result an increment to a tendency for that stimulus to evoke that response.

7. Secondary Motivation

IT IS A MATTER of common observation that situations which are associated with drives themselves become C_D's. Consider, for example, the case involving tissue injury. The response leading to escape from the injury gets connected to the stimuli and to the traces of those stimuli which are associated with the onset of the injury through the resulting cessation in the drive stimulus discharge (S_D) (Postulate III). These antedating stimuli when later encountered will therefore give rise to more or less realistic reproductions of these movements. Now, these antedating stimuli are the new C_D's, and the proprioceptive stimuli activated by the associated internal or "fear" reactions become the S_D's of the *secondary drive* or motivation. Finally, the intensity of this combination of stimuli, especially of the proprioceptive internal or "fear" stimuli, through the principle of stimulus-intensity dynamism (*36*) gives them their distinctive motivational potentiality.

Such acquired associative connections not only have motivational powers, but their diminution or cessation will now possess the power of reinforcement (Postulate III). This is illustrated very nicely by the following experiment reported by Miller (48). Twenty-five albino rats placed in a white chamber were given strong electric shocks which (primary drive) caused them to run at once through a door into an adjoining black compartment where no shocks were received. But the shocks with their following cessations set up in the animals the internal response of fear, so that when later put into the white chamber a few times *without* shock they continued to run into the adjoining black chamber. At this point the connecting door was closed, but a convenient gadget was placed near it which when moved would cause the door to open. Over half of the animals in their random attempts to get through the door moved the gadget and so escaped into the black chamber. The resulting cessation of the white stimulation at once reduced the fear reactions and so the intensity of the internal stimuli constituting the secondary drive or motivation. But a reduction in a drive stimulus discharge (S_D) constitutes a reinforcement of the preceding act (Postulate III). As a result most of the animals which chanced to move the gadget learned to do so more and more quickly, as shown by the graphic representation of the mean reciprocal reaction latencies appearing in Figure 5. Later, when the first gadget ceased to open the door but a second quite different gadget would do so, the first-learned reaction was gradually replaced by the movement of the second gadget by the animals. This demonstrated a second time the functional reality of the secondary (fear) drive or motivation

While Miller's investigation of the fear drive appears at

present to have no experimental parallel which demonstrates the conversion of the sex drive to the status of a secondary motivation, common observation leads strongly to the expectation that a suitably conducted experiment would have an analogous outcome. Let us

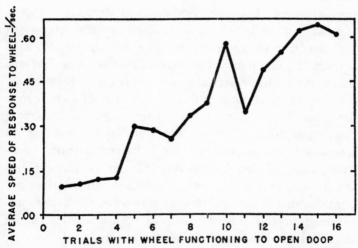

Figure 5. Graphic representation of the process of learning a habit under the influence of a secondary or acquired drive or motivation (fear). Taken from Miller (48, p. 94).

say that the nude body of a sexual partner, coupled with characteristic movements, will evoke tumescence with the accompanying internal stimulation. Now, the diminution of the drive at the orgasm will serve to reinforce an associative connection between the tumescent activity and any neutral stimuli normally present. As a consequence, on later occasions when the hitherto neutral stimuli are encountered they will evoke the tumescence, the stimuli of which will constitute the drive, as before, but now as a secondary or derived motivation.

While not so striking in their manifestations as the two drives just considered, the hunger and thirst drives probably operate in the same general manner. Anderson, working on a theory not very different from that described above (1), has carried out a moderately convincing experiment in which he trained hungry rats to run without error a fairly complex maze with an ordinary food reward (2). He then ran numerous animals on a different maze; the animals were satiated but reward was present. The behavior of these animals is of special significance for secondary motivation, which is called by Anderson, "externalization." It was found that they showed distinct learning as compared with the behavior of control animals; none of them, however, learned as effectively as the hungry rewarded group, though the theory does not demand this. Thus the hunger motivation became conditioned to the general external characteristics of the maze which became the C_D of the hunger drive, i.e., of a secondary motivation, though the tendency was rather weak. Unfortunately, Anderson does not give the statistical reliabilities of his findings.

Finally, it may be added that the understanding of the subject of secondary motivation is rather obscured by the fact that its relationship to incentive motivation, K (pp. 47 ff.), and to the associated mechanisms of anticipatory goal reactions in terms of stimulus-intensity dynamism, V (pp. 41 ff.), has not yet been clarified.

Generalizing on the above considerations, we arrive at the following corollary (30, p. 98):

i. *When neutral stimuli are repeatedly and consistently associated with the evocation of a primary or secondary drive and this drive stimulus undergoes an abrupt diminution, the hitherto neutral stimuli acquire the capacity to bring about the drive stimuli (S_D) which thereby become the condition (C_D) of a secondary drive or motivation.*

8. Secondary Reinforcement

WE NOW PASS from secondary drive, or motivation, to secondary reinforcement. We have seen that secondary drive or motivation is acquired through learning. We must now observe that secondary reinforcement is also acquired through learning. The principle of secondary reinforcement was well known to Pavlov as a fact, and it was used by us as a primary postulate in 1943 (*30*, p. 95). With the additional insight which has come through further research and study by, notably, Spence (*66*), Mowrer (*51*), and Miller (*49*), it becomes evident that a derived or secondary principle may be deduced by a logical process from other primary principles which are available. An informal outline of the essential reasoning follows.

We have seen (p. 20) that whenever a stimulus or stimulus trace is associated with a response and this association is conjoined with a diminution in the drive or motivation (stimulus intensity), an increment to reinforcement (s $\rightarrow$ r) occurs. We must now observe that in a behavior sequence such as that of a rat passing from a compartment where its feet are receiving electric shocks on its way to a non-shock goal or compartment, there occurs a cessation not only of the shock stimuli but of the proprioceptive stimuli arising from the running. This major reduction in stimulation constitutes, of course, the concrete substance of the reinforcement of the running or escape activity, quite as ordinarily aroused. But it also constitutes much more, and this is the main point to observe: the cessation of the shocks not only brings the locomotor escape, but also a general relaxation of the autonomic activity called *fear*. This relaxation process appears to become attached, much as positive activity would, to the stimuli active at the time, together with the traces of earlier stimuli. As a result, on later repetitions of the objective conditions in question this relaxation generalizes forward on those traces, and gives rise to conditioned inhibitions. This has appropriately been called by Miller, *anticipatory relaxation* (*49*).

But relaxation of the muscular contractions reduces proprioceptive stimulus intensity and so reduces the drive stimulus wherever it occurs. And a reduction in the drive does two things: first, it reduces reaction potential and so the speed of locomotion at the time, which is easily observed. This is possibly substantiated by the fact that when animals approach a goal there normally results a rather marked slowing of the locomotion speed, though this could be produced by a combination of other principles (*3; 68*) if the behavior chain has appreciable length. Second, a reduction in drive stimulus constitutes the condition of reinforcement. It follows that any stimulus consistently associated with a reinforcement situation will through that association acquire the power of evoking the conditioned inhibition, i.e., a reduction in stimulus intensity, and so of itself producing the resulting reinforcement. Since this indirect power of reinforcement is acquired through learning, it is called *secondary reinforcement.*

But the fact that the type of reinforcement here under consideration is secondary, in no way suggests that it is unimportant. Actually the great mass of our everyday acts are initiated by secondary drives, and the most of civilized human learning apparently is effected through secondary reinforcement. Presumably the tension (anxiety) over the success of an anticipatory recall in rote learning which occurs when the syllable comes into view is the reinforcing agent there involved (*38*) The click of the food-release mechanism in Skinner's experiment (*64*) served as the reinforcing agent (*30*, p. 88). The sight of the grains of boiled rice in Grindley's experiment (*16*) served to reinforce the locomotor reaction of his chicks even for a time when they received no food (*30*, p. 92). The click of the food-release mechanism in Bugelski's experiment (*5*) yielded enough reinforcement to delay the progress of the experimental extinction (*30*, p. 91). And Cowles' chimpanzees (*7*) received secondary reinforcement from their possession of the colored tokens which would later be inserted into a vending machine and exchanged for a raisin (*30*, p. 90). Miller (*49*) has given an elaborate tabulated analysis of a dozen or more additional cases of analogous nature.

Generalizing on the preceding considerations, we arrive at the following corollary (*30*, p. 95):

ii. *A neutral receptor impulse which occurs repeatedly and consistently in close conjunction with a reinforcing state of affairs, whether primary or secondary, will itself acquire the power of acting as a reinforcing agent.*

9. The Law of Habit Formation ($_8H_R$)

WE SAW ABOVE (pp. 15 ff.) that the "law" or fact of reinforcement states the *conditions* under which habits are formed. Here, on the other hand, we are to consider the quantitative law of habit formation as a function of the *number* of reinforcements involved.

Strictly speaking, a habit is never observed as such, since it is hidden in the nervous system of the subject. We can observe the habit only indirectly by observing the molar (macroscopic) behavior of its possessor as it is mediated by previously formed habits. This means that habit ($_8H_R$) is a symbolic construct. The true nature of the concept will be clarified by the procedure utilized in the determination of the quantitative law. This is as follows:

Ideally, about 200 organisms should be trained under constant conditions of drive, and so forth, by distributed reinforcement on some simple act, the latency, intensity, amplitude, or some other quantitative aspect of the response being taken at each trial. These quantifications of the responses of the separate individuals are then subjected to the paired-comparisons procedure (*39*). From

these pooled results are computed the reaction potentials
($_sE_R$) at 25 or so trials suitably scattered throughout
the learning process. Such a set of reaction potentials is
represented by the circles shown in Figure 6.

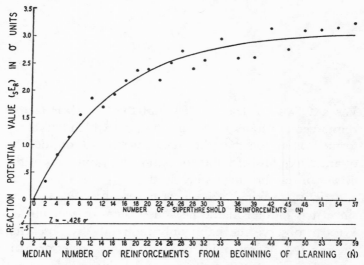

Figure 6. Graphic representation of the functional relationship of
reaction potential ($_sE_R$) as derived by the method of objective quantitative paired comparisons of the reaction latencies ($_{st}R$) of 59 albino
rats reinforced with a food pellet once every 24 hours under a drive
(D) of 22 hours' food privation. The broken line represents an extrapolation of the equation originally fitted to the $_sE_R$ values represented
by the black circles, to what purports to be the absolute zero (Z) of
reaction potential. Reproduced from Figure 1 of Gladstone *et al.* (*13*).

The next thing is to determine the quantitative law of
these reaction potentials by finding the equation which
fits the numerical data as well as possible, i.e., with the
least mean square deviation from the empirical values.
Actually an exact fit to such data from a moderate

number of subjects cannot be expected. Moreover, the equation-fitting process has two objectives: one is to identify the form of the equation most probably represented by the data; the other is to determine the numerical values of one or more "constant" terms which chance to appear in the best-fitting type of equation. Such a fitted equation is represented by the smooth curve which runs among the circles shown in Figure 6. The equation in question is (13, p. 515):

$$_sE_R = 3.55(1 - 10^{-.0305\dot{N}}). \qquad (4)$$

It is to be noted that equation 4 as it stands is not, strictly speaking, an equation of $_sH_R$ as a function of the number of reinforcements. Actually, as we shall show presently (pp. 33 ff.), the coefficient (3.55) seems to be anything but an expression of habit strength. However, the remainder of the right-hand member of the equation, being clearly dependent upon the number of reinforcements ($\dot{N}$), is evidently an expression of habit strength. We are accordingly able, anticipating the evidence to be presented later (pp. 57 ff.), to write the equation for habit formation:

$$_sH_R = 1 - 10^{-.0305\dot{N}}. \qquad (5)$$

It is to be noted further that this equation or formula furnishes the natural basis for a centigrade system of representing habit magnitudes. For example, when the following sets of $\dot{N}$'s at the left are substituted in equation 5, they yield the $_sH_R$ values shown at the right:

if $\dot{N} = 0$, $_sH_R = .0000$,
if $\dot{N} = 2$, $_sH_R = .1312$,
if $\dot{N} = 4$, $_sH_R = .2453$,

$$\text{if } \dot{N} = 20, \, _sH_R = .7546,$$
$$\text{if } \dot{N} = 41, \, _sH_R = .9438,$$
$$\text{if } \dot{N} = \infty, \, _sH_R = 1.0000.$$

The point is that habit strength varies from zero to 1.00 as a total range. Obviously, if .01 is taken as the unit of habit magnitude, or *hab*, there will be a total range of 100 habs from the least to the greatest possible habit strength. This of course is a simple and natural centigrade quantification.

Generalizing on the preceding considerations, we arrive at the following postulate:

IV. If reinforcements follow each other at evenly distributed intervals, everything else constant, the resulting habit will increase in strength as a positive growth function of the number of trials according to the equation,

$$_sH_R = 1 - 10^{-a\dot{N}}.$$

In an analogous manner we arrive at the following definition:

The hab is a centigrade unit of habit strength extending by steps of .01 from zero to 1.00.

10. Primary Motivation or Drive (D) with Habit Strength ($_sH_R$) Acting Jointly, Other Factors Constant

THERE EXIST in varying degrees certain conditions in the body, such as the lack of nutrition, water, or oxygen, the ample presence of the appropriate sex hormone, tissue injury of various sorts, and any stimulation beyond certain intensities; these constitute conditions of primary drive (C_D). Drive itself (D) is a quantitative intervening variable lying between the C_D and the response (R). Ordinarily these drive conditions, if intense enough, release innate behavioral activities ($_sU_R$) which tend to rectify the biological emergency involved. Even when very weak they "motivate" habits, particularly those which in the past have been associated with these or similar conditions. As a rule the vigor of the response evoked is a positive increasing function of the intensity of the condition which sets it in motion. For example, the vigor of an animal's struggle for food or water increases, other things equal, with the number of hours of food or water privation up to the point of beginning weakness from inanition.

Now it happens that this factor of drive also emerges from the equational analyses utilized above in the study of the law of habit formation (p. 31). For example, Perin reports the learning of a simple bar-pressing habit by two groups of albino rats (56). One group, in an ex-

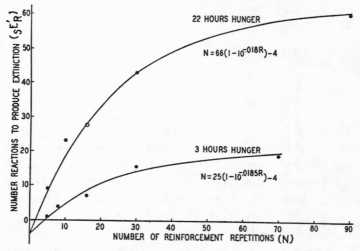

Figure 7. Two parallel learning curves showing the different reaction potentials ($_sE_R'$) when drives of different intensity are operating. Adapted from Perin (56).

periment which Perin himself performed, was under a 3-hour hunger drive; the second group, in an experiment performed by Williams (75), was under a 22-hour hunger drive. In reporting their studies these authors utilized the number of unreinforced reaction evocations (n) instead of $_sE_R$, because these values are quantitatively somewhat similar to $_sE_R$ and the true $_sE_R$ determination was not available at the time. As an expository device, we accordingly use the symbol $_sE_R'$ instead of either.

The two sets of learning data are graphically represented on this basis as sequences of circles in Figure 7. Equations analogous to equation 4 above (p. 31) were fitted to these data and are represented graphically by the smooth lines running among the two circle sequences. They are respectively

$$_sE_R' = 66(1 - 10^{-.0180N}) - 4$$

and

$$_sE_R' = 25(1 - 10^{.0185N}) - 4.$$

It will be noticed that in these equations the exponential "constants" (.0180 and .0185) are presumably alike except for variability due to sampling limitations, whereas the coefficients (66 and 25) are radically different. This suggests that the parts of the equations which are nearly alike are so because of the empirical conditions which are alike, and that the parts of the equations which are different are so because of the empirical conditions which are different. As a matter of fact, we shall have occasion to utilize this type of analysis, especially the part involving differences, repeatedly during the next few sections. At this point we conclude that the coefficients in these two equations (66 and 25) express a quantification (and isolation) of the drive component involved, much as the parenthetical parts represent the habit component. It may be noted, incidentally, that in these equations *the multiplication of the habit component* ($_sH_R$) *by the drive component* (D) *produces the reaction potential* ($_sE_R'$), i.e.,

$$_sE_R = f(_sH_R \times D). \qquad (6)$$

Clearly, if enough of such coefficient isolations of sufficiently different but comparable drives were available from equations fitted to such empirical values, they should yield, when properly fitted by equations involving the conditions which produce the drive, a first approximation to the law of drive (D) as a function of the drive conditions (C_D), e.g., of the number of hours of food

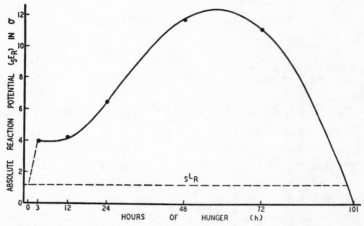

Figure 8. Graphic representation of the reaction potential produced by varying drive conditions with habit strength constant. Each circle represents the indirect determination of $_sE_R$ on a separate group of albino rats. The broken line represents in a general way the results obtained by several investigations in a region of h values not covered by Yamaguchi's experiment represented by the circles, and is added as a simple expository device. Adapted from a figure used by Yamaguchi (78).

privation (h). As a matter of fact, something like this was done by Perin. His data (30, p. 228, Figure 49) substantially verified results found by previous workers (Figure 8, 64; 72), but the range of his privation conditions (1 to 23 hours) was too small for the detailed determination of such a complex function.

Yamaguchi made a special investigation of this problem, which covered food privations ranging from zero hours to three days and involved two distinct experiments (78). The results of one of his experiments are represented by the circles in Figure 8. Unfortunately, from the point of view of expository consistency, these values were not obtained by the straightforward procedure recommended in the preceding paragraph, but indirectly through computations based on distinct empirical equations, including $_8E_R = f(n)$ and $n = f(h)$. Even so the graph agrees substantially with preceding studies (56; 64; 72). It shows at first a rise in $_8E_R$ with positive acceleration which inflects at around h = 30, rises to a somewhat surprising maximum of 12.3 σ at around h = 59, after which it falls as starvation begins to weaken the drive. The portion of the curve from h = 72 to h = 101 is, of course, an extrapolation and as such is less significant than the rest. Thus in the food-privation drive Yamaguchi finds that two factors are involved: (1) the drive itself (D) which, taken alone, is an increasing monotonic sigmoid function; this is multiplied by (2) a negative or inanition factor, which after four days or so produces death in these animals. The two factors appear clearly in the equation fitted to these five data, which is:

$$D = (37.824 \times 10^{-27.496\frac{1}{h}} + 4.001)$$
$$(1 - .00001045h^{2.486}). \quad (7)$$

In equation 7 the first parenthesis (D') represents the drive component proper, whereas the second parenthesis (ϵ) represents the negative or inanition component.

Generalizing on the preceding considerations, we arrive at part A of our next postulate (30, p. 253):

V. A. Primary motivation (D), at least that resulting from food privation, consists of two multiplicative components, (1) the drive proper (D′) which is an increasing monotonic sigmoid function of h, and (2) a negative or inanition component (ϵ) which is a positively accelerated monotonic function of h decreasing from 1.0 to zero, i.e.,

$$D = D' \times \epsilon.$$

It will be observed that in Figure 8 the smallest h value represented by the data circles has a value of 3 hours. It happens that the extreme range of h values between zero and 3 hours has been investigated independently by Koch and Daniel (43), by Saltzman and Koch (63), and by Yamaguchi in a separate unpublished study. All three experiments show that there is a sharp break in the D function at about 3 hours. For reasons not entirely clear, Perin's results show no indication of this break even at one hour of food privation. The weight of the experimental results therefore indicates that in this region D falls in approximately a straight line to a very low value, i.e., approximately to the reaction threshold ($_SL_R$), though probably not quite to it. As an expository device, a broken line is for this reason added to Figure 8, though the data involved come from three different experiments.

Generalizing on the above considerations, we arrive at part B of our postulate:

V. B. The functional relationship of drive (D) to one drive condition (food privation) is: from h = 0 to about 3 hours, drive rises in a linear manner until the

function abruptly shifts to a near horizontal, then to a concave-upward course, gradually changing to a convex-upward curve reaching a maximum of 12.3σ at about h = 59, after which it gradually falls to the reaction threshold ($_8L_R$) at around h = 100.

It will be recalled (p. 5) that the central coördinating neural apparatus must connect the responding mechanisms with the nature and extent of the need. Evidently this is ordinarily achieved by means of stimuli (S) which are initiated by the C_D, presumably in the case of hunger as an increasing function of the number of hours of food privation. This type of stimulation we shall in general call S_D. Apparently an S_D accompanies all true drives as an increasing function of their intensities. It may be noted incidentally that the principle of stimulus-intensity dynamism (V) (pp. 41 ff.) implies that S_D has appreciable dynamic or moving, i.e., motive, powers in its own right which are closely related to primary motivation. This serves to recall Miller's hypothesis in this regard (*50*, p. 18 ff.).

Generalizing on the above considerations, we arrive at part C of our postulate (*30*, p. 253):

V. C. Each drive condition (C_D) generates a characteristic drive stimulus (S_D) which is a monotonic increasing function of this state.

And finally it must be pointed out that primary motivations are not entirely independent but tend to summate with, or generalize to, each other to an appreciable extent (*30*, p. 248). The *a priori* probability of such a state of affairs is represented by the view that at zero food privation the reaction potential has an appreciable strength, if one or more of certain other drive conditions are operating. This may possibly be due at least in part to the stimulus generalization of the one S_D to the other, or to secondary motivation (p. 24), or to both combined.

Actually, since this idea was originally put forward (*30*, pp. 284 ff.), several studies have produced evidence which indicates that alien drives do in fact influence positively the reaction potential of habits set up under quite different drives. For example, Webb (*73*) trained rats to open a door to get a pellet of food for a total of 90 trials with 22 hours' food privation and zero hours' water privation. Then the response was extinguished with food satiation but with water privation in various degrees. The extinction results indicate that the presence of the alien water drive had an appreciable tendency to motivate the habit set up on the basis of food. Miller (*49*) reports somewhat similar results on hunger motivating a water-based habit, and on pain motivating a habit based on food. And Felsinger found that the presence of the female sex hormone in ovariectomized rats produced a greater amount of eating and drinking during these extinction processes respectively than when the hormone was absent (*11*, p. 51).

Generalizing on the preceding considerations, we arrive at part D of our postulate (*30*, p. 253):

V. D. At least some drive conditions tend partially to motivate into action habits which have been set up on the basis of different drive conditions.

11. Stimulus-Intensity Dynamism (V) with Habit Strength ($_sH_R$) Acting Jointly, Other Factors Constant

IN CONTINUING THE STUDY of the joint action of various factors leading to the production of reaction potential, we now add to those just considered a third factor—stimulus intensity (53). The essential logic of this situation is perhaps best presented by an unpublished experiment carried out in the writer's laboratory by Ruth Hays, in 1946. Two groups of 20 albino rats each were trained to jump over an 8.5-inch gap for food, in a modified Lashley jumping apparatus possessing only a single stimulus object. One group jumped against a black cardboard door swinging from the top, and the other jumped against a similar white door. The latencies ($_st_R$'s) of the jumps were automatically recorded.

The animals made 11 reinforced jumps on each of 13 days. There was found to be a rather abrupt warming-up tendency following the first trial during the early stages of learning, and generalization tests were inserted on the eighth trial on some days. There accordingly remained only the latency scores for trials 2 to 7 inclusive upon which to base learning curves. The reciprocals of the means of these six daily sets of latencies were calculated for the respective groups of animals as the nearest approximation to reaction potential available. These values are represented by the circles in Figure 9. Equa-

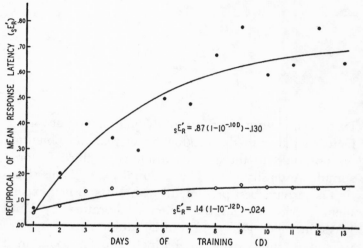

Figure 9. Graph representing learning curves of rats jumping to two different stimulus intensities, black (lower curve) and white (upper curve). The D's in the equations represent reinforcement days. From an unpublished study performed in the writer's laboratory by Ruth Hays.

tions have been fitted to each of these two sets of learning data. They are represented by the smooth curves running among the respective circle sequences. While the divergence of the data points from the curves representing the fitted equations, especially the upper one, is marked, the two sets of data are clearly distinct. The accent marks are placed on the $_s E_R$'s because, while latency reciprocals approximate reaction potentials closely enough for illustrative purposes, they are not true $_sE_R$'s.

A brief inspection of Figure 9 together with the corresponding equations seems to indicate (1) that the numerical part of the exponents of the expressions representing the process of habit formation ($_sH_R$) as a function of the number of reinforcements (.10 and .12) remains constant except for sampling limitations; (2) that the coefficients (.14 and .87) increase clearly as the stimulus-intensity dynamism (V) increases from black to white, drive held constant; and (3) that *reaction potential ($_sE_R$) is produced by the multiplication of the stimulus-intensity component (V) by that of habit strength ($_sH_R$)*, i.e.,

$$_sE_R = f(V_2 \times {}_sH_R), \qquad (8)$$

where V_2 is based on the stimulus intensity which *evokes* the response.

But in a really quantitative science we require a knowledge of the mathematical or functional relationship of reaction potential ($_sE_R$) to stimulus intensity (S). So far, no one seems to have investigated the law of stimulus-intensity dynamism (V) for its own sake, so that we have as yet very inadequate evidence regarding the functional relationship. If a half dozen or more of the coefficients such as are yielded by the Hays data were available, an equation could be fitted to them as a function of the corresponding stimulus intensities involved, but two such paired values are far too few for such a purpose. However, a certain amount of incidental evidence from reaction-time studies is available, where the $_sH_R$ factor presumably is near its maximum of 1.00 and therefore constant. Piéron (59) has published some excellent results of this type, involving both hearing and taste; and Cattell, years ago, published a somewhat similar study in the field of vision (6). Naturally none of these data was in terms of reaction potential, all having been reported as reaction latencies ($_s t_R$).

In an attempt to secure an approximation to the law of reaction potential as a function of stimulus intensities, the reaction latencies for Cattell's two subjects were averaged and then converted into equivalent reaction potentials by means of the modified form of an equation which recently became available (13, p. 517). The outcome of this procedure indicated the probability that Cattell's unit, while suitable for his own purposes, was not fine enough for ours. By assuming that his unit was 12.5 times the size of the stimulus limen and adjusting his published data to this smaller unit, we secure the numerical data represented by the circles in Figure 10. The smooth line drawn through these data points represents the equation

$$_s E_R = 1.328(1 - 10^{-.440 \log S}). \tag{9}$$

It is assumed that the motivation or drive in the Cattell study was secondary for his human subjects (14; 18; 20), and that it was constant. The point is that a series of coefficients such as those would, on curve-fitting analysis, presumably again split up into two factors—the one represented by the parenthesis (equation 9) corresponding to stimulus-intensity dynamism (V) as such, i.e.,

$$V = 1 - 10^{-.440 \log S}, \tag{10}$$

and still another coefficient, 1.328. It is noteworthy that the values of V vary from zero to a maximum of 1.00, and so this function falls naturally into a centigrade system somewhat like $_sH_R$.

At this stage of our exposition we must point out that stimulus-intensity dynamism has an important influence

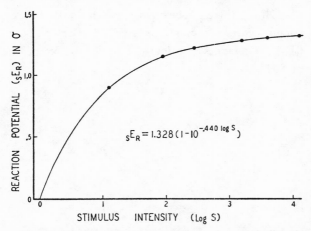

Figure 10. Graphic representation of some indirectly obtained reaction potential values, together with a smooth curve representing an equation fitted to the data as a function of the intensities of the stimuli involved. Graph adapted from Hull (36). Original data from Cattell (6).

on habit formation of a multiplicative nature. This is expressed in the following equation:

$$_s\dot{H}_R = {}_sH_R \times V_1, \tag{10'}$$

where V_1 represents the stimulus intensity involved in the original learning.

But what is the significance of this emerging coefficient of 1.328 in equation 9? For one thing it presumably includes the drive (D) which is present even though held constant. What else may be implicit within it should be revealed in due course by further application of the equation-fitting type of analysis considered above.

Generalizing on the preceding considerations, we arrive at the following postulate:

VI. Other things constant, the magnitude of the stimulus-intensity component (V) of reaction potential ($_8E_R$) is a monotonic increasing logarithmic function of S, i.e.,

$$V = 1 - 10^{-a \log S}.$$

12. Incentive Motivation (K) with Habit Strength ($_sH_R$) Acting Jointly, Other Factors Constant

PURSUING OUR OBJECTIVE of isolating the various factors which contribute to the determination of reaction potential, we turn now to an experimental analysis of the role of incentive. The best study so far available in this field was carried out by Crespi (8). Here, exactly as in the analysis of the role of stimulus intensity (p. 41), the study of incentive begins with the determination of the approximate equivalent of the reaction potential as a function of the number of reinforcements. In Crespi's case the nearest equivalent of reaction potential available at the time was the reciprocal of the reaction time, i.e., the speed of locomotion in feet per second. He plotted this as a function of the amount, or weight (w), of the food incentive given as reinforcement to albino rats deprived of food for a constant period of 22 hours. A typical and illuminating outcome of this type of procedure is shown in Figure 11. An equation was fitted to each of these learning curves by Bengt Carlson. The equations are as follows, the accent marks above the E's indicating

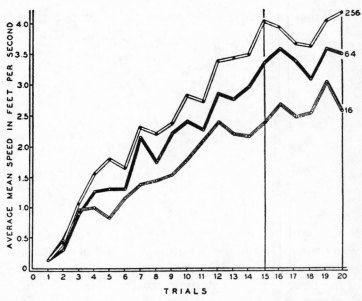

Figure 11. Graph representing learning curves with the same *number* of reinforcements with three different *magnitudes* of incentive, i.e., food reinforcement. Reproduced from Crespi (*8*, p. 488).

that the values involved are approximations to $_sE_R$'s (speeds of locomotion in feet per second) instead of the result of the paired-comparisons procedure.

$$_sE_R' = 5.653(1 - e^{-.0662N})$$
$$_sE_R' = 5.407(1 - e^{-.0558N})$$
$$_sE_R' = 4.134(1 - e^{-.0572N}).$$

An inspection of the curves shows that the asymptotes increase as the amount of food (in fiftieth grams) is increased. A glance at the corresponding equations shows, just as in the case of Perin's results, that the numerical constants in the three exponents are about the same, the variation here also possibly being due to sample-size limitations. On the other hand, the coefficient representing the fitted asymptotes varies systematically with variation in the incentive magnitude (w), as already suggested by the graphs. Here once again the parentheses are relatively similar, presumably because the number of reinforcements are alike, and the coefficients are different because the corresponding incentives are different. Accordingly we conclude that the parentheses represent habit strength and the coefficients represent the incentive factor. Moreover, it is also to be observed that *reaction potential involves the multiplication of the incentive component (K) by habit strength* (*30*, p. 178), i.e.,

$$_sE_R = f(K \times {}_sH_R). \tag{11}$$

As in the two preceding sections of the empirical analysis of $_sE_R$ (D and V), our program calls for the fitting of an equation to the coefficients of the several learning curves as a function of the incentive weight (w). Once more, however, the available data while more complete still are inadequate since only three of the five learning curves were adequate for equation fitting. Omitting the outcome of the test score at zero incentive as presumably distorted upward by frustration, we have taken the remaining five empirical asymptote values presented in Crespi's published data (*8*, p. 494). They are represented graphically in Figure 12. The three highest data points correspond to the coefficients of the equations shown on page 48, except that all have considerably smaller values. An equation has been fitted to these results as a function of the weight of the corresponding incentive given as reinforcement. By this procedure we obtain the following relationship:

$$_{s}E_{R} = 5.1(1 - 10^{-.120\sqrt{w+1}}) - 1.14. \qquad (12)$$

This is represented by the smooth curve running among the data points. For our present purposes the

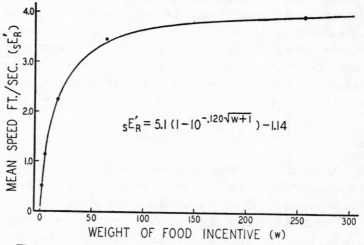

Figure 12. Graphic representation of the asymptotes of five learning curves as a function of the weight (w) of food used as incentive or reinforcement. The smooth line running among the asymptotic circles represents an equation fitted to those values. Based on data published by Crespi (8, p. 494). This corresponds to Crespi's Figure 1, 9, p. 344.

−1.14 may presumably be ignored. This leaves us with the parenthesis involving the incentive, for which we may write the following equation:

$$K = 1 - 10^{-.120\sqrt{w+1}}. \qquad (13)$$

A simple inspection of this K factor shows that it will

vary from zero toward 1.00, and so is a centigrade function.

There still remains the 5.1 of equation 12 to be identified. Presumably this represents the variables held constant in the experiment, namely, the near-maximum habit strength ($_sH_R$) and drive (D) at 22 hours of food privation. This means that if the experiment had also varied in a systematic manner the number of hours of hunger, the same type of analysis would have yielded a systematic increase in those coefficients with the increase in the number of hours of food privation exactly as Perin's study did.

Generalizing on the above considerations, we arrive at the following postulate (*30*, p. 178):

VII. The incentive function (K) is a negatively accelerated increasing monotonic function of the weight (w) of food given as reinforcement, i.e.,

$$K = 1 - 10^{-a\sqrt{w}}.$$

13. Delay in Reinforcement (J) with Habit Strength ($_sH_R$) Acting Jointly, Other Factors Constant

CONTINUING OUR ANALYSIS of the factors which contribute to the determination of reaction potential, we proceed to consider the influence of delay in the presentation of the incentive, i.e., in reinforcement. In this field a great deal of excellent experimental work has been done during recent years variously under the names of the "goal gradient" (24) and the "gradient of reinforcement," especially in K. W. Spence's laboratory (66; 67; 15; 58). Very little of this material can be utilized for our present purposes, however, because the results are complicated by the alternative responses involved in trial and error. Moreover, in the one study by Perin (57) which is not complicated by trial and error, the results have been published as median reaction latencies.

Fortunately we now have an equation (13) by which latencies may be converted into reaction potentials. But this equation,

$$_sE_R = 2.845(_st_R)^{-.483} - .599, \tag{14}$$

even though secured by use of practically the same apparatus as that used by Perin, involves considerably smaller latencies than his experiment did. In order to secure a somewhat better approximation to $_sE_R$'s from Perin's latency data, the 2.845 and the .599 in the above equation are both multiplied by 2; this yields the equation

$$_sE_R = 5.690(_st_R)^{-.483} - 1.198.$$

The learning was attained in Perin's experiment by the movement of a simple bar (much as in the Felsinger experiment from which equation 14 was derived), following which the food reinforcement was administered after delays of 0, 2, 5, 10, and 30 seconds respectively. However, the animals did not learn at 30 seconds' delay, which seems to mean that the function passes below zero before 30'' delay.

Substituting Perin's published median latencies in this equation we presumably secure a fair approximation to the corresponding $_sE_R$ values for four learning curves. These are represented in Figure 13. There it may be seen at once that as the delay in reinforcement increases, the reaction potentials of the approximate asymptotes of the several curves are correspondingly *decreased*.

In order to secure an objective determination of the values both of these asymptotes and of the exponential constants relatively uncomplicated by sampling limitations, equations have been fitted to the data of the respective learning curves. These are shown in Figure 13 adjacent to the curves in question. Despite a considerable amount of deviation from the fitted curves in all four cases, the fits are well separated. An examination of these equations reveals a phenomenon not previously observed clearly, namely, that the steepness of the rise of the learning curves as shown by the magnitude of the exponential constants (.0245, .0216, .0177, and .0096) obviously is not constant. Instead it appears to be a consistently decreasing function of the amount of delay in reinforcement.

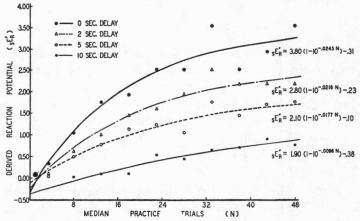

Figure 13. Learning curves showing the influence of delay in reinforcement, other factors constant, on the accumulation of reaction potential during 50 practice trials of a simple bar-pressing act. The $_sE_R$ values here represented were calculated from median reaction latencies ($_st_R$) published by Perin (57).

This suggests that the exponent may ultimately also be expressed as a function of the delay in reinforcement. If this tendency is verified it will evidently complicate the interpretation now to be made.

The coefficients of these equations indicate the fitted asymptotes. With four of these available, even though in terms of $_sE'_R$, we evidently have identified a quantitative factor dependent upon delay in reinforcement, which is quite analogous to what we have found in the cases of D, V, and K already considered. We accordingly proceed at once to the determination of the quantitative law involved. This is shown graphically in Figure 14, where the

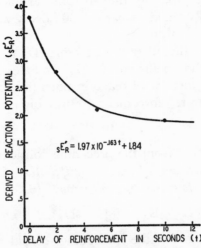

Figure 14. Graphic representation of the effect of delay in reinforcement (J) on the asymptotes of learning curves as a function of the magnitude of the delay in reinforcement. Plotted from the coefficients of the fitted equations shown in Figure 13.

asymptotes of the several curves are represented by circles as a function of the corresponding seconds of delay in reinforcement. An equation which fits these data fairly well is

$$_{s}E_{R} = 1.97 \times 10^{-.163t} + 1.84, \qquad (15)$$

which may be considered as an approximation to the law

of reaction potential as a function of delay in reinforcement with other factors constant. It is believed, however, that the fact that the falling function lacks 1.84σ of reaching the reaction threshold (as shown by the equation and Figure 14) is probably due to some artifact, since the animals totally failed to learn at $30''$ delay which clearly is beneath the threshold.

Presumably the other three factors (D, V, and K) are implicit in the coefficient (1.97). It follows from this analysis that the law of reaction potential as a function of the delay in reinforcement presumably is

$$J = 10^{-.163t}. \qquad (16)$$

It is also evident from the preceding considerations that *reaction potential results from the multiplication of a function of the delay in reinforcement by habit strength* (*30*, p. 178), i.e.,

$$_sE_R = f(J \times {}_sH_R). \qquad (17)$$

Generalizing on the preceding considerations, we arrive at the following postulate (*30*, p. 178):

VIII. The greater the delay in reinforcement, the weaker will be the resulting reaction potential, the quantitative law being:

$$J = 10^{-jt}.$$

14. The Constitution of Reaction Potential ($_sE_R$)

IN EACH of the five preceding sections we have presented evidence purporting to indicate the quantitative molar law according to which habit strength ($_sH_R$), primary motivation or drive (D), incentive motivation (K), stimulus-intensity dynamism (V), and the delay in reinforcement (J) respectively operate as functions in the determination of reaction potential. Moreover, in the four preceding sections, equations 6, 8, 11, and 17 have indicated that habit strength is combined with each of the other four processes in the evolution of reaction potential in a multiplicative manner. These four functional equations are as follows:

1. $_sE_R = f(D \times {_sH_R})$.
2. $_sE_R = f(V_2 \times {_sH_R})$.
3. $_sE_R = f(K \times {_sH_R})$.
4. $_sE_R = f(J \times {_sH_R})$.

Now the manner of the derivation of these four multiplicative functional equations suggests strongly that all five of the components probably combine to produce reaction potential by the simple process of multiplication, i.e., that

$$_8E_R = D \times V_2 \times K \times J \times {}_8H_R. \qquad (18)^*$$

Orienting ourselves a little further regarding the factors composing $_8E_R$, we find that D alone as yielded by the analysis has a maximum magnitude presumably differing with different primary drives but in the case of hunger ranging uncertainly from 6 to 12σ. In some sense this may be considered the basic or major magnitude in the composition of $_8E_R$. Secondly, it may be observed that the remaining four magnitudes (V_2, K, J, and $_8H_R$) are essentially decimals, ranging from zero to 1.0. This means that as these latter values are multiplied together the product in general tends to grow smaller and smaller. Thus, if each of these four should stand at .85 their product would be about .522, and this multiplied by 6σ would yield 3.13σ, a value not very different from the values secured in a number of experimental determinations (*13; 74; 78*). Moreover, equation 18 implies that if any one of the five functional values (including secondary motivation under the symbol D) should be zero, $_8E_R$ would itself become zero quite as indicated by ordinary observation (*60*).

It may be added that the nature of the method employed in the preceding analysis of the determiners of reaction potential furnishes no certainty that the above list exhausts the factors constituting reaction potential. All we can say is that these are all we have been able to

---

* This equation assumes that D, V, K, and J remain constant during learning and response evocation. It is not general enough to cover cases where changes are made in these factors during the experiment.

identify so far as operative in ordinary learning. In this connection see related note, pages 122 ff.

Generalizing on the preceding considerations, we arrive at the following postulate (*30*, p. 178):

IX. The reaction potential ($_8E_R$) of a bit of learned behavior at any given stage of learning, where conditions are constant throughout learning and response evocation, is determined (1) by the drive (D) operating during the learning process multiplied (2) by the stimulus-intensity dynamism of the signaling stimulus in response evocation (V_2), (3) by the incentive reinforcement (K), (4) by the gradient of delay in reinforcement (J), and (5) by the habit strength ($_8\dot{H}_R$), i.e.,

$$_8E_R = D \times V_2 \times K \times J \times {_8\dot{H}_R,} \qquad (19)$$

where

$$_8\dot{H}_R = {_8H_R} \times V_1,$$

and where V_1 is that involved in the original learning.

15. The Problem of the Behavioral Summation ($+$) of Habit Strengths ($_sH_R$)

IT SOMETIMES HAPPENS that a given response (R) is conditioned to a stimulus (S) and that later the same response is conditioned to a second stimulus (S') on the same generalization continuum. Let us assume that the S' $\dashrightarrow$ R connection receives 6 reinforcements; that the S $\dashrightarrow$ R connection receives 10 reinforcements; that the generalization differences (d) between S and S' is 7 units; that

$$_{S'}H_R = 1 - 10^{-.0305\dot{N}}; \tag{5}$$

and that

$$_S\bar{H}_R = {}_{S'}H_R \times 10^{-.0135d}. \tag{20}$$

The first step in the procedure is to calculate the habit strength attached to S' by substituting appropriately in equation 5:

$$_{S'}H_R = 1 - 10^{-.0305 \times 6}$$
$$= 1 - 10^{-.1830}$$
$$= 1 - \frac{1}{1.524}$$
$$\therefore {}_{S'}H_R = .34384.$$

Next, substituting .34384 and 7 in equation 20, we secure the stimulus generalization of $_sH_R$ from S' to S:

$$_s\bar{H}_R = .34384 \times 10^{-.0135\times7}$$
$$= .34384 \times 10^{-.0945}$$
$$= .34384 \times \frac{1}{1.243}$$
$$\therefore \; _s\bar{H}_R = .2766.$$

But .2766 is the generalization of S' to S. This means that at that point, according to equation 20,

$$.2766 = 1 - 10^{-.0305\dot{N}}.$$

From this we can calculate the equivalent number of trials it *would* have required to produce this habit strength *de novo* at S. Solving for $\dot{N}$, we have

$$1 - .2766 = \frac{1}{10^{.0305\dot{N}}}$$
$$.7234 = \frac{1}{10^{.0305\dot{N}}}$$
$$10^{.0305\dot{N}} = \frac{1}{.7234}$$
$$.0305\dot{N} = \log 1.3823$$
$$\dot{N} = \frac{.14019}{.0305}$$
$$\therefore \; \dot{N} = 4.5964.$$

If, now, we add to the equivalent of an $\dot{N}$ of 4.5964, ten more reinforcements, we have a total of $\dot{N} = 14.5964$. Substituting this in equation 5, we secure what purports to be the sum of the habit strengths from the two distinct sources:

$$_8H_R = 1 - 10^{-.0305 \times 14.5964}$$
$$= 1 - 10^{-.44519}$$
$$= 1 - \frac{1}{2.787}$$
$$\therefore \ _8H_R = .6412,$$

which is what we have been seeking.

As a matter of fact, the same end can be obtained directly from the two habit strengths involved. Substituting 10 for the $\dot{N}$ in equation 5 and solving, we secure an $_8H_R$ value of .50446, which presumably would have been yielded by 10 reinforcements at S *de novo*. Next, the values of this $_8H_R$ and the $_8\overline{H}_R = .2766$ produced by stimulus generalization receive behavioral summation by means of Perkins' equation (*27*, pp. 20, 21):

$$_8H_R \dotplus {_8\overline{H}_R} = {_8H_R} + {_8\overline{H}_R} - \frac{_8H_R \times {_8\overline{H}_R}}{M}.$$

Substituting in this equation, recalling that the growth limit of $_8H_R$ (as now quantified) is 1.00 (which we can subsequently neglect), we have

$$_8H_R \dotplus {_8\overline{H}_R} = .50446 + .2766 - \frac{.50446 \times .2766}{1.00}$$
$$= .78106 - .13953$$
$$\therefore \ _8H_R \dotplus {_8\overline{H}_R} = .64153,$$

which checks with the ($\dotplus$) value secured above except for dropped decimals.

Generalizing on the preceding considerations, we arrive at the following corollary (*30*, p. 223):

iii. *If two stimuli, S′ and S, are reinforced separately to a response (R) by Ṅ′ and Ṅ reinforcements respectively, and the $_{s'}H_R$ generalizes to S in the amount of $_sH'_R$, the summation (+̇) of the two habit strengths at S will be the same as would result from the equivalent number of reinforcements at S, i.e.,*

$$_sH_R \mathbin{\dot{+}} {}_sH'_R = {}_sH_R + {}_sH'_R - {}_sH_R \times {}_sH'_R. \qquad (21)$$

16. The Problem of Behavioral Summation ($+$) in Terms of Reaction Potential ($_sE_R$)

WE ASSUME the same situation regarding habit strengths as in the preceding section. From Postulate IV, we have

$$_sH_R = 1 - 10^{-a\dot{N}}, \tag{5}$$

and from Postulate IX, we have

$$_sE_R = D \times V_2 \times K \times J \times {}_s\dot{H}_R. \tag{19}$$

Letting $D \times V_2 \times K \times V_1 \times J = M$, and substituting equation 5 in equation 19, we have

$$_sE_R = M(1 - 10^{-a\dot{N}}),$$

which in current symbolism is Perkins' basic assumption (*27*, p. 20), and from which he derived the equation for the summation of reaction potentials (*27*, p. 21):

$$_sE_R + {}_s\underline{E}_R = {}_sE_R + {}_s\underline{E}_R - \frac{_sE_R \times {}_s\underline{E}_R}{M}. \tag{22}$$

Assuming that $M = 5.0\sigma$, we can easily illustrate the use of equation 22 by the example used in the preceding section:

$$_8E_R = {_8}H_R \times M = .50446 \times 5.0 = 2.52230.$$
$$_8\underline{E}_R = {_8}\bar{H}_R \times M = .27660 \times 5.0 = 1.38300.$$
$$_8E_R + {_8}\underline{E}_R = ({_8}H_R + {_8}\bar{H}_R)M = .64153 \times 5.0$$
$$= 3.20765.$$

Or, substituting the values of $_8E_R$ and $_8\underline{E}_R$ in equation 22, we have

$$_8E_R + {_8}\underline{E}_R = 2.52230 + 1.38300 - \frac{2.52230 \times 1.38300}{5}$$
$$= 3.9053 - .69766$$
$$= 3.20764,$$

which agrees with the value secured from $({_8}H_R + {_8}\bar{H}_R)M$ just above, except for dropped decimals.

Generalizing from the above considerations, we arrive at our next corollary:

iv. *If two stimuli, S' and S, are reinforced separately to a response (R), and $_{S'}E_R$ generalizes to S in the amount of $_8E'_R$, the two reaction potentials will summate at S as would the equivalent number of reinforcements in an original learning, i.e.,*

$$_8E_R + {_8}E'_R = {_8}E_R + {_8}E'_R - \frac{{_8}E_R \times {_8}E'_R}{M}.$$

17. The Problem of Behavioral Withdrawal ($\div$) in Terms of Habit Strength ($_sH_R$)

LET US ASSUME the same general situation as in the preceding two sections except that here the habit situation is in reverse. For convenience in representation we let $_sH_R \dotplus _sH_R' = C$. It follows from equation 21 that

$$_sH_R + _sH_R' - _sH_R \times _sH_R' = C.$$
$$_sH_R - _sH_R \times _sH_R' = C - _sH_R'.$$
$$_sH_R = \frac{C - _sH_R'}{1 - _sH_R'}. \qquad (23)$$

For example, we assume as above that

$$_sH_R = .50446$$
$$_sH_R' = .27660$$
$$C = _sH_R \dotplus _sH_R' = .64153.$$

Substituting these values in equation 23, we have

$$_8H_R = \frac{.64153 - .27660}{1 - .27660}$$
$$= \frac{.36493}{.72340}$$
$$= .50446,$$

which agrees with the value of $_8H_R$ as given above, within the limits of dropped decimals.

Generalizing from these considerations, we have our next corollary:

v. *If a small habit strength $(_8H'_R)$ is to be withdrawn $(\div)$ from a larger habit strength (C), the result will be*

$$C \div {_8H'_R} = {_8H_R} = \frac{C - {_8H'_R}}{1 - {_8H'_R}}$$

18. The Problem of Behavioral Withdrawal ($\div$) in Terms of Reaction Potential ($_s E_R$)

LET IT BE ASSUMED that we have a reaction potential to the amount of C and we wish to withdraw ($\div$) $_s E_R'$ from it. We have by equation 22

$$_s E_R + {_s E_R'} - \frac{{_s E_R} \times {_s E_R'}}{M} = C,$$

and we wish to find

$$C \div {_s E_R'} = {_s E_R}.$$

Clearing the fraction in the above equation, we have

$$M_s E_R + M_s E_R' - {_s E_R}_s E_R' = MC$$
$$M_s E_R - {_s E_R}_s E_R = MC - M_s E_R'$$
$$_s E_R(M - {_s E_R'}) = M(C - {_s E_R'})$$
$$\therefore {_s E_R} = \frac{M(C - {_s E_R'})}{M - {_s E_R'}}. \quad (24)$$

For example consider the concrete situation mentioned in connection with Corollary iv, where

$$C = 3.20764,$$
$$M = 5.0,$$
$$_8E_R' = 1.38300,$$

and

$$_8E_R = 2.52230.$$

Substituting the values of C and $_8E_R$ in equation 24, we have

$$_8E_R = \frac{5.0(3.20764 - 1.38300)}{5.0 - 1.38300}$$
$$= \frac{9.12320}{3.6170}$$
$$= 2.52231,$$

which agrees with $_8E_R$ within the limits of dropped decimals.

Generalizing on the above considerations, we arrive at our next corollary:

vi. *If a small reaction potential* $(_sE_R')$ *is to be withdrawn* $(\div)$ *from a larger reaction potential* (C), *the result will be*

$$_8E_R = C \div {_8E_R'} = \frac{M(C - {_8E_R'})}{M - {_8E_R'}}.$$

19. The Problem of the Behavioral Summation (+) of Incentive Substances (K)

IT MAY HAPPEN that several incentives are employed simultaneously in a given bit of learning. For example, when water is mixed with pulverized dog food to make a rewarding pellet for rats, and the subject is both hungry and thirsty, presumably both the food and the water combine as simultaneous incentives. The experimental determination of the law of this combination is an attractive prospect. As a preliminary survey of the empirical potentialities, the following elaboration is presented.

Even though some water was added by means of an atomizer to Crespi's pellets just before they were used, we may, for expository purposes in this place, take his results as the general basis in the consideration of food only. Accordingly let us assume that the functional law of the food incentive alone is

$$K_f = 1 - 10^{-A\sqrt{w}}, \qquad (13')$$

where w represents a weight measured in .02 gm. units. Also for expository reasons, let us assume that a parallel experiment based on water (aqua) yielded the functional outcome

$$K_a = 1 - 10^{-B\sqrt{m}},$$

where the unit of m is one cubic milligram of ordinary water, say. Now it is fairly plausible to assume that the values of different simultaneous incentives combine like comparable amounts of the same incentive. Nevertheless there still remains the important question as to the method of determining the amount of water, however measured, that will be equal in incentive power to one unit of food.

It is evident from an inspection of the two preceding equations that whatever the units involved, and whatever the relative potencies of the incentive substances, when the product of the two components of the exponent $A\sqrt{w}$ is equal to that of the two components of $B\sqrt{m}$, the values of the respective K's will be equal. Therefore when the two K's are in fact equal we can write the equation

$$A\sqrt{w} = B\sqrt{m}.$$

Solving for the value of w, we have

$$\sqrt{w} = \frac{B}{A}\sqrt{m}$$

$$\therefore w = \frac{B^2}{A^2}m. \tag{25}$$

Suppose, now, that $A = .12$, that $B = .18$, and that $m = 3$ units. Substituting this in equation 25, along with the numerical exponential values, we have

$$w = \frac{.18^2}{.12^2} \times 3$$

$$= \frac{.0324}{.0144} \times 3$$

$$= 2.25 \times 3$$

$$\therefore w = 6.75.$$

In other words, 3 units of water, on these assumptions, would be equal to 6.75 units of food.

Now let it be assumed that the 3 units of water are added to 20 of the food units per trial. From the preceding this would be equivalent to adding 6.75 units of food. This would make an equivalent total of $20 + 6.75$, or 26.75 units of food per trial. Substituting the 26.75 in equation 13', we have

$$K_f = 1 - 10^{-.12\sqrt{26.75}}$$

$$= 1 - 10^{-.12 \times 5.172}$$

$$= 1 - 10^{-.62064}$$

$$= 1 - \frac{1}{4.175}$$

$$\therefore K_f = .76048.$$

In short, the 20 food units and the 3 water units purport having been combined here in the joint determination of a single incentive motivation.

Generalizing on the preceding considerations, we arrive at the following corollary:

vii. *If two incentive substances, f and a, have $A \sqrt{w}$ and $B \sqrt{m}$ as the exponential components of their respective functional equations, the second substance will combine $(+)$ with the first in the production of the total K according to the following equation:*

$$K_{f+a} = 1 - 10^{-A\sqrt{w + m \times \frac{B^2}{A^2}}}.$$

20. Inhibitory Potential

THERE HAS BEEN implicit in the preceding presentation of the acquisition of habit strength and reaction potential (pp. 15 ff.) the fact that often stimuli' are incidentally associated with reinforcements which have nothing to do with the essential cause of the reinforcement. This means that such stimuli will tend to acquire a power to evoke the R, but if they do so by themselves the reinforcement will not follow; i.e., adaptively this $_8E_R$ will be in error and therefore false. The molar principle which mediates the correction or elimination of this and analogous forms of false reaction potentials is experimental extinction. Looking still more closely at the process here involved, we find underlying it a variable of considerably wider application which is called *inhibitory potential* (I_R). This is believed to be a residual or after-effect left, apparently, by all responses (R), which is in the nature of a negative drive akin to tissue injury, fatigue, or "pain." It tends to inhibit that reaction potential, i.e., to prevent the occurrence of the response in question and possibly other responses.

Generalizing on the preceding considerations, we arrive at part A of Postulate X (*30*, p. 300):

X. A. Whenever a reaction (R) is evoked from an organism there is left an increment of primary negative drive (I_R) which inhibits to a degree according to its magnitude the reaction potential ($_sE_R$) to that response.

But inhibitory potential (I_R) has a marked tendency to dissipate spontaneously with the passage of time. Experimental work by Ellson (*10*) has shown indirectly that this occurs approximately according to a simple decay function. Generalizing on these considerations, we arrive at the next portion of our postulate (*30*, pp. 271, 275):

X. B. With the passage of time since its formation, I_R spontaneously dissipates approximately as a simple decay function of the time (t) elapsed, i.e.,

$$I_R' = I_R \times 10^{-at}.$$

We have seen above (p. 20) that the diminution in a drive is one of the necessary conditions of reinforcement, i.e., of habit formation. By Postulate X B, there results a reduction in a particular I_R as soon as the activity which produced it ceases, the amount of reduction being a function of the I_R present at the time. As pointed out by Neal Miller (*49*, p. 40), this reduction is especially marked in respect to the afferent proprioceptive impulses which are akin to tissue injury coming from the effectors in question at once after the cessation of the activity, i.e., the beginning of rest. Moreover, Kimble (*42*, p. 22) implies that the magnitude of $\Delta_s I_R$ is an increasing function of the loss in I_R due to rest, and so of the amount of I_R present at the time. The organic response process most closely preceding this drive reduction would be the cessation of the activity itself. In accordance with the principle of reinforcement, the cessation or reduction of this activity in the presence of I_R would condition the latter to any stimuli or stimulus traces accompanying or shortly preceding the resting state (*49; 51*).

Generalizing on the preceding considerations, we arrive at the following corollary (*30*, p. 300):

viii. *Stimuli and stimulus traces closely associated with the cessation of a given activity, and in the presence of I_R from that response, become conditioned to this particular non-activity, yielding conditioned inhibition ($_sI_R$) which will oppose $_sE_R$ involving this response, the amount of $\Delta_s I_R$ generated being an increasing function of the I_R present.*

There has been implicit in the immediately preceding exposition the assumption that increments of inhibition (ΔI_R) occurring in close succession summate in considerable amounts, and that the conditioned inhibition ($_sI_R$) generated in appreciable amounts as this goes on is summated with the I_R into an inhibitory aggregate ($\dot{I}_R$). Unfortunately we do not yet have precise evidence as to the quantitative law of these summations ($\dotplus$).

Generalizing qualitatively, we arrive at the next portion of our postulate (*30*, p. 285):

X. C. If responses (R) occur in close succession without further reinforcement, the successive increments of inhibition (ΔI_R) to this response summate to attain

appreciable amounts of I_R. They also summate with $_sI_R$ to make up an inhibitory aggregate $(\dot{I}_R)$, i.e.,

$$\dot{I}_R = I_R \dotplus {_sI_R}. \tag{26}$$

General confirmation of the above postulate (C), as well as empirical illustration of the functions of $\dot{I}_R$ and I_R, is presented in a study published by Kimble (42, p. 20). Eight groups totaling 474 human subjects learned a special alphabet-printing task; one group learned by distributed trials, one group, by massed trials, and six groups, by massed training for varying numbers of trials. Following this a ten-minute rest period was inserted, after which training was resumed. Now, by definition,

$$_s\bar{E}_R = {_sE_R} - \dot{I}_R. \tag{27}$$

Substituting for $\dot{I}_R$ the corresponding value of equation 26, we have

$$_s\bar{E}_R = {_sE_R} - ({_sI_R} \dotplus I_R).$$

Since the I_R spontaneously dissipates and $_sI_R$, being a habit, presumably does not dissipate appreciably, the rest period will permit a partial spontaneous dissipation of $\dot{I}_R$. If the rest period were long enough to permit all the I_R to dissipate, the residue would be $_sE_R$ and pure $_sI_R$, leaving

$$_s\bar{E}_R = {_sE_R} - {_sI_R}. \tag{28}$$

This dissipation of I_R represents an appreciable increase in $_s\bar{E}_R$, called *spontaneous recovery*. Now the learning by distributed trials represents a minimum of both I_R and $_sI_R$, i.e., an approximation to pure $_sE_R$. But since, by transposing equation 28, we have

$$_sE_R - {_s\bar{E}_R} = {_sI_R},$$

the difference between this $_sE_R$ and the approximate $_s\bar{E}_R$ after a rest period should yield a value which is mainly a function of conditioned inhibition, i.e., $_sI_R$ in approximate isolation. A curve of the rise of $_sI_R$ as a function of the number of practice trials plotted on this general

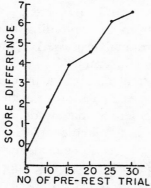

Figure 15. An approximate learning curve of conditioned inhibition ($_sI_R$) as a function of the amount of training. Reproduced from Kimble (*42*, p. 20).

basis may be seen as Figure 15. It shows a fair approximation to a typical learning curve.

At this point we approach the phenomenon of experimental extinction, which requires certain preliminary considerations. Now, by definition, assuming that no inhibitory potential ($\dot{I}_R$) is present, the superthreshold reaction potential ($_s\dot{E}_R$) is that portion of it which lies above, i.e., exceeds, the reaction threshold ($_sL_R$). This means that

$$_s\dot{E}_R = {_sE_R} - {_sL_R}. \qquad (29)$$

When $\dot{I}_R$ has increased until it equals $_S\dot{E}_R$, we have, by definition,

$$\dot{I}_R = \dot{I}_R.$$

And when

$$_S\dot{E}_R - \dot{I}_R = 0, \tag{30}$$

experimental extinction is complete.

It is evident from the preceding that experimental extinction is a gradual process. We must accordingly raise the question concerning the law of the increase of the $\dot{I}_R$ as the ordinal number of unreinforced reaction evocations ($\dot{n}$) succeed each other in the case of a particular reaction potential magnitude. We are fortunate in having such a determination (74). Thirty-six albino rats each received 40 reinforcements in walking 8 inches and pushing under a light, sloping door to secure food. Since the animals required very uneven numbers of trials to extinguish, all the latency series were reduced to the equivalent of the median number of reactions to extinction (44) by an equally weighted Vincent method (28, p. 245) as a first approximation to 36 animals, all naturally extinguishing at that number of reaction evocations. Then the adapted Thurstone method of paired comparisons (39) was applied to 26 strategically located sets of these Vincentized latencies, the same as in the case of the determination of reaction potential described above (p. 12). This of course yielded the gradual weakening of $_S\dot{E}_R$ as it was progressively neutralized by $\dot{I}_R$ down to $_S\dot{L}_R$. The equation fitted to these $_S\dot{E}_R$ values as a function of the ordinal sequence of extinction trials ($\dot{n}$) was (74),

$$_S\bar{E}_R = 1.84 \times 10^{-.0434\dot{n}} + .277. \tag{31}$$

Actually it is an easy matter to convert these $_s\bar{E}_R$ data into $\dot{I}_R$ values by adding together the scale-value differences yielded by the scaling procedure, only starting with zero at the beginning of the extinction process instead of

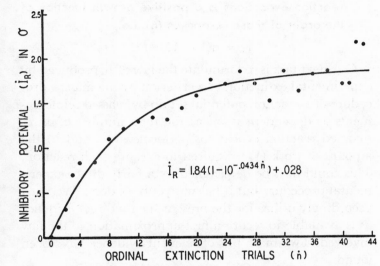

Figure 16. Graphic representation of the progressive increase in $\dot{I}_R$ with the successive massed unreinforced evocations ($\dot{n}$) of the response R leading to complete extinction. These data were secured from the published values of $_s\bar{E}_R$ by subtracting each of them from the maximum range of the scaled data. Derived from Wilcoxon, Hays, and Hull (74).

at its termination. The $\dot{I}_R$ values so secured are shown in detail in Figure 16. For similar reasons equation 31 can be rewritten in the form of a positive growth function which fits the $\dot{I}_R$ data to exactly the same extent:

$$\dot{I}_R = 1.84(1 - 10^{-.0434\dot{n}}) + .028. \qquad (32)$$

Generalizing on these considerations, we arrive at Part D of Postulate X:

X. D. When experimental extinction occurs by massed practice, the $\dot{I}_R$ present at once after the successive reaction evocations is a positive growth function of the order of those responses ($\dot{n}$), i.e.,

$$\dot{I}_R = a(1 - 10^{-b\dot{n}}).$$

Our next task is to formulate the law of $\dot{I}_R$ produced by experimental extinction to a criterion by the massed procedure of a reaction potential set up by massed reinforcements as dependent upon a) the total number of unreinforced reaction evocations performed (n), and b) the amount of work (W) required to execute each reaction. This could now be determined by a fairly direct experimental procedure but it has not yet been done. We must accordingly utilize for the present such indirect evidence as is available to secure a first approximation to the law involved. Two main bits of relevant evidence have been found.

1. Mowrer and Jones (52) determined the number of reaction evocations (n) required to produce experimental extinction on three comparable groups of albino rats trained to near maximum habit strength by massed trials to press a bar for food reward. During extinction the bars of the respective groups were weighted differently, requiring widely varying amounts of work. The equation fitted to these data is (30, p. 300)

$$n = 373 - 3.2 \text{ gm.,}$$

which may be rewritten

$$n = 373(1.0 - .00857W),$$

in which the 373 apparently represents the maximum n producible by the Mowrer-Jones special extinction procedure with a zero weight and near-maximum $_8H_R$. With a weight of 15 gm., used by Perin, this equation becomes

$$n = 325(1.1476 - .00984W). \tag{33}$$

Generalizing on the preceding considerations, we arrive at the final portion of Postulate X, recalling equation 29 (30, pp. 280, 300):

X. E. For constant values of superthreshold reaction potential ($_8\dot{E}_R$) set up by massed practice, the number of unreinforced responses (n) producible by massed extinction procedure is a linear decreasing function of the magnitude of the work (W) involved in operating the manipulanda, i.e.,

$$n = A(a - bW).$$

2. Williams (75) and Perin (56) trained a total of five groups of 40 albino rats each, to press a 15-gram bar for food pellets by differing numbers of reinforcements (N). The reaction potentials at 23 hours' hunger were computed from these five N's together with an N of zero, which represents an approximation to the reaction threshold ($_8L_R$) or zero n. An equation fitted to these six values of $_8E_R$ as a function of n is

$$_8\dot{E}_R = 4.00(1 - 10^{-.0114n}).$$

Transforming this we have

$$n = -87.7 \log (1 - .25_8\dot{E}_R). \tag{34}$$

The value of this n corresponds approximately to the

325 of equation 33. Substituting the value of n appearing in equation 34 in place of the 325 seen in equation 33, we have

$$n = [-87.7 \log (1 - .25_s E_R)](1.1476 - .00984W). \quad (35)$$

But since by equation 30, $_s E_R = \dot{I}_R$, equation 35 becomes

$$n = [-87.7 \log (1 - .25 \dot{I}_R)](1.1476 - .00984W). \quad (36)$$

We proceed now to determine $\dot{I}_R$ as a function of W for a constant n which we will take at 30. We do this by substituting a series of W values, e.g., 0, 5, 15, 20, 40, 60, 80, and 100 grams, and some others in equation 36 along with a constant n of 30. For example, we take W with a value of 40. Substituting in equation 36 and solving for $\dot{I}_R$, we have

$$[-87.7 \log (1 - .25 \dot{I}_R)](1.1476 - .25 \times 40) = 30$$

$$\log (1 - .25 \dot{I}_R) = -\frac{30}{66.1258} = -.4537$$

$$1 - .25 \dot{I}_R = 10^{-.4537} = .3517$$

$$-.25 \dot{I}_R = -1 + .3517 = -.6483$$

$$\therefore \dot{I}_R = \frac{.6483}{.25} = 2.5932.$$

Substituting the other W values in turn we conclude with the calculated values represented by the circles in Figure 17. Clearly, $\dot{I}_R$ rises at first with a positive acceleration as W increases, then passes into a negatively accelerated phase, soon becoming asymptotic. It is especially to be noted that when W = 0, the $\dot{I}_R$ for 30 responses is about half as great as at the maximum of 110 grams. While a part of this may easily be due to the unreliability of the constants involved, it doubtless represents a substantial amount of work (W) produced by the mere movement of the bodily parts involved. This opens up a fascinating field of research in the determination of the amount of work involved in the mere movement of the body incidental to the performance of that on the

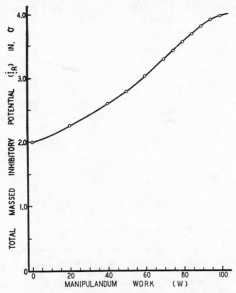

Figure 17. A quantitative theoretical representation of inhibitory potential ($\dot{I}_R$) as a function of the work (W) of operating the manipulandum, the number of unreinforced reactions required to produce total experimental extinction (n) remaining constant at 30.

manipulandum as such. A manipulandum of near zero W could be constructed by requiring the animal to move its paw between a suitably prepared pair of light rays.

Generalizing on the preceding considerations, we arrive at the following corollary:

ix. *For a constant value of n, the inhibitory potential* $(\dot{I}_R)$
*generated by the total massed extinction of reaction potentials
set up by massed practice begins as a positively accelerated increasing function of the work* (W) *involved in operating the
manipulandum, which gradually changes to a negative accelera-*

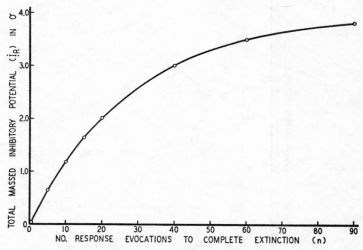

Figure 18. A quantitative theoretical representation of inhibitory
potential, $\dot{I}_R$, as a function of the number of unreinforced reaction
evocations required to produce total experimental extinction (n) of
reaction potentials set up by massed reinforcements, the work (W)
of operating the manipulandum remaining constant at 40 grams.

*tion at around 80 grams, finally becoming asymptotic at around
110 grams.*

Finally we consider inhibitory potential as a function
of the number (n) of the reactions evoked in producing
total experimental extinction, the work of operating the
manipulandum now being constant. This is done by
first taking W at 40 grams, simplifying the right-hand

member, then substituting for n 0, 5, 10, 15, 20, 40, 60, and 90 in succession, and solving for $\dot{I}_R$, exactly as above. Thus we arrive at the values represented by the data points shown in Figure 18, which reveals an exponential or growth function of n.

Generalizing on the preceding considerations, we arrive at the following corollary:

x. *For a constant value of the work (W) involved in operating the manipulandum, the inhibitory potential ($\dot{I}_R$) generated by the massed total extinction of reaction potentials set up by massed practice is a negatively accelerated increasing function of the total number of reactions (n) required.*

21. Stimulus Generalization, $_s\underline{E}_R$ and $_s\underline{I}_R$

WHEN A STIMULUS (Ṡ) is connected with a response (R) in a learning situation, not only that stimulus acquires a capacity to evoke the response, but other adjacent stimuli on the same stimulus continuum also acquire this capacity, though to a diminishing degree (35). This is illustrated by a study reported by Hovland (21). Twenty human subjects were conditioned to give a galvanic skin reaction to a tone. Then the tone was tested for its power of evoking this response along with three other tones separated from the first by 25, 50, and 75 j.n.d.'s in pitch. The results are shown by the four data points in Figure 19. This presents a clear decay function which is fairly well fitted by the equation

$$_s\underline{E}'_R = 12.3 + 6 \times 10^{-.0135d}. \tag{37}$$

It is believed that the reason the generalized response approximation (measured in millimeters) to reaction potential ($_s\underline{E}'_R$) does not have an asymptote of zero is that only one component of the stimulus complex conditioned to the response is changed in the generalization determination—namely, that of pitch. The various inci-

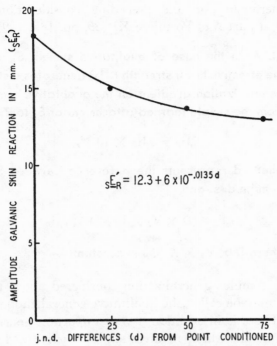

Figure 19. Graphic representation of the gross stimulus generalization gradient based on vibration frequency as a function of the j.n.d.'s from the conditioned stimulus to the evoking stimuli. Plotted from data published by Hovland (*21*).

dental stimuli which consistently occur at the same time also become connected to the response and evoke it whenever any part of the generalization continuum occurs, giving a false appearance of generalization. This presumably makes up the 12.3 of equation 37. It means that the true generalization portion of this equation probably is that enclosed within the parenthesis.

Generalizing on the preceding considerations, we arrive at part A of Postulate XI (*30*, pp. 185, 199):

XI. A. In the case of qualitative stimuli, S_1 and S_2, the effective habit strength ($_s\bar{H}_R$) generates a stimulus generalization gradient on the qualitative continuum from the simple learned attachment of S_1 to R:

$$_{s_2}\bar{H}_R = {}_{s_1}H_R \times 10^{-ad}, \tag{38}$$

where d represents the difference between S_1 and S_2 in j.n.d.'s, and

$$_{s_2}\underline{E}_R = D \times V_2 \times K \times J \times {}_{s_1}\bar{H}_R,$$

where $D \times V_2 \times K \times J$ is constant.

The stimulus generalization considered above is that which may be called the qualitative generalization function. There is in addition a very important generalization function which involves stimulus *intensity*. The investigations by Hovland (*22*) and Brown (*4*) have shown that stimulus intensity also has a special type of generalization gradient which falls more steeply when extending toward weaker stimuli than toward stronger stimuli. It is also noteworthy that this type of gradient seems to begin, at least superficially, with complete generalization. These phenomena appear to be caused by (1) the fact that the gradients involve V as a variant as well as $_s\bar{H}_R$, and (2) the fact that incidental stimuli (see XI A) produce a strong appearance of horizontal generalization which, by summation ($+$), gives the appearance of a flattened gradient whose asymptote is far above zero.

Generalizing on the preceding considerations, we arrive at part B of our postulate (*30*, pp. 186, 199):

XI. B. A stimulus intensity (S_1) generalizes to a second stimulus intensity (S_2) according to the equation

$$_{s_2}\bar{H}_R = {_{s_1}}H_R \times 10^{-bd},$$

where d represents the difference between S_1 and S_2 in log units, and

$$_{s_2}E_R = ({_{s_1}}H_R \times V_2)(D \times K \times J),$$

where ($D \times K \times J$) is constant and V_2 is the stimulus-intensity dynamism at S_2.

Part B, together with the principle of the drive stimulus (S_D), evidently implies that there will be a falling-off gradient in the reaction potential when a shift is made from the drive intensity at which a habit was originally established to a different drive intensity. This implication will, of course, be complicated by the principle of stimulus-intensity dynamism, which accounts for the consistent evidence (*40*) of both types of S_D generalization gradient found by Yamaguchi (*78*). This is shown graphically in Figure 20. It should be observed that in each of these graphs the factor which is varied is found in the *training* conditions and that the test conditions are held constant, whereas the usual practice in stimulus generalization experiments (e.g., Figure 19) is to hold the training conditions constant while varying the *test* conditions. Yamaguchi's procedure prevents an artifact in the generalization function from the action of stimulus-intensity dynamism. Note that in general the 72-hour test yields an appreciably higher $_sE_R$ value than does the 3-hour test, which is to be expected on the basis of this V factor.

Generalizing on the preceding considerations, we arrive at the following corollary (*30*, p. 244):

xi. *When a habit is set up in association with a given drive intensity and its strength is tested under a different drive intensity, there will result a falling gradient of $_s\bar{H}_R$ and $_s\underline{E}_R$.*

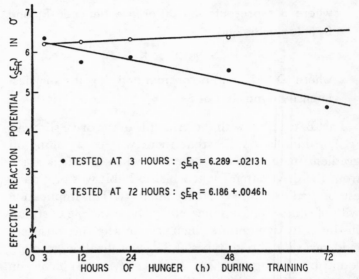

Figure 20. Graphs representing two generalization gradients based on drive intensities of the food-privation variety. From Yamaguchi (*78*).

At this point we turn to the analogous situation involving $_sI_R$ which, as pointed out above (pp. 76 ff.) is regarded as a kind of negative habit. In that case it is to be expected that stimulus generalization would be operative as with any other habit phenomenon. As a matter of fact, the expectation is realized. This is also illustrated by Hovland's study, already cited. Using the same stimuli

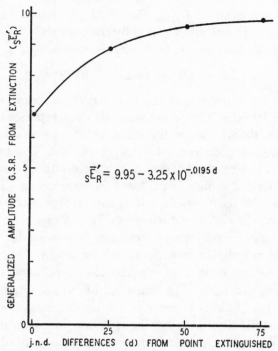

Figure 21. Graphic representation of the gross stimulus generalization gradient of the results of experimental extinction at one point (0) in relation to other reinforced points (1, 2, and 3), as subtracted from a uniform basic functional approximation to reaction potential, $_s\bar{E}'_R$. Plotted from data published by Hovland (27).

as those described above, Hovland set up conditioned galvanic skin reactions on *each* of the four pitch stimuli, then partially extinguished the extreme stimulus in the series, and, finally, tested the response-evocation intensity at all four points. The means from 20 human subjects

are shown graphically in Figure 21. An equation fitted
to these data and represented by the smooth line running
among the four points in the figure is

$$_8\bar{E}'_R = 9.95 - (3.25 \times 10^{-.0195d}). \qquad (39)$$

It will be noticed that the curve rises, whereas that of
Figure 19 falls. This is because the data represent a difference, that between the basic reaction potential and
the recently acquired inhibitory potential. The latter is
represented by the portion of the right-hand member of
the equation which is enclosed in parenthesis. This, if
graphed by itself, would fall as d increases. Accordingly
$_8\bar{E}'_R$, i.e., the difference, rises as d increases.

Actually, experimental evidence is lacking for determining whether the generalized factor in the case of
experimental extinction is really $_8I_R$ or $\dot{I}_R$, even though
a resting procedure like that used by Kimble mentioned
above (p. 76) should serve to clarify the matter without
much difficulty. Meanwhile we state our postulate in
terms of $_8I_R$, even though it may quite possibly turn out
to be $\dot{I}_R$.

Generalizing on the preceding considerations, we arrive at part C of our postulate (30, p. 264):

**XI. C. In the case of qualitative stimulus differences,
ordinary conditioning and extinction spontaneously
generate a gradient of inhibitory potential ($_8I_R$)
which is a negative growth function of $_8I_R$ and d, i.e.,**

$$_{8_2}I_R = {_{8_1}}I_R \times 10^{-ad}, \qquad (40)$$

and in the case of stimulus-intensity differences,

$$_{8_2}I_R = {_{8_1}}I_R \times 10^{-bd} \times V_2.$$

22. Afferent Stimulus Interaction

FOR SOME TIME there has been a fairly general belief that an interaction occurs between the afferent impulses (s) evoked by stimuli (S) acting on the receptors at close to the same time. Pavlov, the Russian reflexologist, seems to have been the first to put forward the hypothesis (*54*, p. 70), but Köhler, the German-American *Gestalt* psychologist, has emphasized it most extensively (*44*, p. 132; *45*, p. 55). Nevertheless the notion is as yet a relatively new one and despite its presumptive ultimate importance has not, as such, attracted the attention of American experimentalists.

Like other internal and directly unobservable states, afferent stimulus interaction is a construct and must be observed indirectly. Since it is a change allied to stimulation, it naturally is revealed as would be a change in stimulation such as pitch just considered, i.e., by a loss in $_sE_R$ analogous to that observed in stimulus generalization. In order to consider this concept more specifically, we will use the following hypothetical example: Let it be assumed that a reaction potential was based on an afferent impulse, s, arising from S, and that later s was changed to š by the interaction caused by the afferent impulse s' from the concurrent action of an otherwise behaviorally neutral stimulus, S'. In case the presence of the additional (neutral) stimulus should increase the joint stimulus-intensity dynamism (V) of the resulting compound situation, suitable corrections presumably could be made by means of equation 25 (p. 71). Let it further be assumed that the original reaction potential of $_*E_R$ was 5σ by specific quantification, based for example upon its latency (p. 106), whereas that of $_*E_R$ has fallen (through stimulus generalization) to 4σ, as shown by a parallel determination.

Now, the best evidence we have on the principle of stimulus generalization (equation 38) indicates that in the present case

$$_*E_R = {}_*E_R \times 10^{-jd}, \tag{41}$$

where j is taken from the qualitative generalization phenomena of the same S, here arbitrarily assumed to be .0135, and d represents the number of j.n.d.'s separating s from š. Substituting in equation 38, we have

$$4\sigma = 5\sigma \times 10^{-.0135d}$$
$$.0135d = \log \frac{5\sigma}{4\sigma}$$
$$d = \frac{\log 1.25}{.0135}$$
$$\therefore d = 7.1785.$$

This means that the afferent interaction effect in the present hypothetical case should be readily possible of determination. Specifically, the external inhibition effects of the presence of the extra stimulus should amount to a little over 7 j.n.d.'s, which would be a quantification of the specific stimulus afferent interaction involved. Thus we would seem to have a typical molar methodology for the quantification of this phenomenon as well as a unit; and the quantificational methodology amounts to a fairly precise operational definition of the phenomenon in question. Nevertheless, the utilization of the quantificational methodology is as yet largely programmatic, and much empirical work remains to be done (*33*). Even now, however, the concept alone gives us a useful behavioral understanding of the essential value of the patterning of stimuli, a secondary principle which evidently plays a critical role in many subtle adaptive phenomena (*30*).

Generalizing on the preceding considerations, we arrive at the following primary behavioral principle or postulate (*30*, p. 47):

XII. All afferent impulses (s's) active at any given instant mutually interact, converting each other into š's which differ qualitatively from the original s's so that a reaction potential ($_sE_R$) set up on the basis of one afferent impulse (s) will show a generalization fall to $_šE_R$ when the reaction (R) is evoked by the other afferent impulse (š), the amount of the change in the afferent impulses being shown by the number of j.n.d.'s separating the $_sE_R$'s involved according to the principle,

$$d = \frac{\log \dfrac{_sE_R}{_šE_R}}{i}. \qquad (42)$$

23. Behavioral Oscillation

ONE OF THE MOST UNIVERSAL OBSERVATIONS of even fully trained acts is that their performance varies from moment to moment. This was recognized and necessarily utilized by the earliest psycho-physicists. This means that reaction potential ($_sE_R$) is subject (*30*, pp. 304 ff.) to momentary oscillation ($_sO_R$). With the recent development of a method for the quantification of reaction potential it is possible to determine in a fairly direct manner the nature of the distribution of these oscillating $_sE_R$ values (*79*). Five thousand such values are represented in Figure 22. Rather precise computations show that although this distribution resembles the normal probability distribution of Gauss, it actually differs to a certain extent in being leptokurtic in form. There are a larger relative number of values in the middle of the distribution, and at the same time a relatively wider dispersion on the sides. So far as available evidence goes, the distribution is probably quite symmetrical.

Generalizing on the above considerations, we arrive

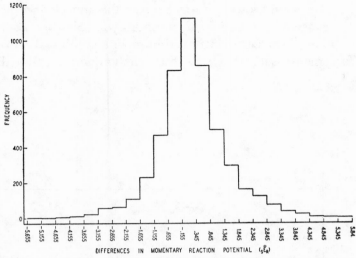

DIFFERENCES IN MOMENTARY REACTION POTENTIAL ($_s\dot{E}_R$)

Figure 22. Graphic representation of behavioral oscillation ($_sO_R$), a distribution of 5000 momentary reaction potential differences ($_s\dot{E}_R$) calculated from the reaction latencies of 59 albino rats following the completion of learning. Reproduced from Yamaguchi *et al.* (*79*, p. 220).

at the first portion of our postulate on this subject (*30*, p. 319):

> XIII. A. Reaction potential ($_sE_R$) oscillates from moment to moment, the distribution of $_sO_R$ deviating slightly from the Gaussian probability form in being leptokurtic with β_2 at about 4.0; i.e., the distribution is represented by the equation (*55*, p. lxiii)

$$y = y_0 \frac{1}{\left(1 + \dfrac{x^2}{a^2}\right)^m}.$$

A question growing at once out of the above concerns the range of this leptokurtic variability as $_sH_R$ (and $_sE_R$) increases from zero to its maximum with continued reinforcement. Earlier (38; 30) this function was postulated

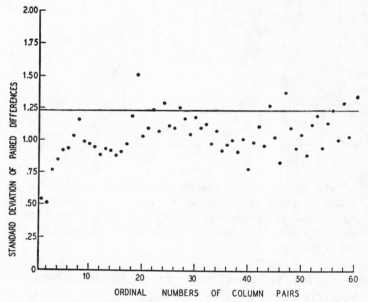

Figure 23. Graphic representation of the magnitude of $_sO_R$ dispersions as a function of the ordinal number of superthreshold reinforcements (N) in terms of the standard deviation of the $_s\acute{E}_R$'s of 59 albino rats while learning a simple habit. Reproduced from Yamaguchi et al. (79, p. 233).

as constant. However, in the recent investigation mentioned above the function was determined empirically throughout the entire range of some 60 learning trials. The results are shown graphically in Figure 23. There it may be seen that the dispersion of $_sO_R$ is by no means constant as learning progresses. In general it increases from first to last, but in irregular waves. Theoretically, in some ways the most important region is at the beginning. Here it may be seen that the first seven super-threshold trials (N) show a very rapid rise in dispersion. If a curve should be drawn through these values and projected backward it is evident that it would cut the base-line at around two trials less than the conventional zero. Now it happens that this is the number of the trials marking the true zero (*13*, p. 514). This would seem to point to a zero dispersion of $_8O_R$ at zero $_8H_R$, whatever the drive (D) may be.

Generalizing on these considerations, we arrive at part B of our postulate (*30*, p. 319):

XIII. B. The oscillation of $_8E_R$ begins with a dispersion of approximately zero at the absolute zero (Z) of $_8H_R$, this at first rising as a positive growth function of the number of superthreshold reinforcements (N) to an unsteady maximum, after which it remains relatively constant though with increasing variability.

To the above we must add part C of our postulate (*30*, pp. 309, 319):

XIII. C. The oscillations of competing reaction potentials at any given instant are asynchronous.

Since the dispersion of $_8O_R$ is the unit of quantification of $_8E_R$ in the present system, the variability revealed by Figure 23 suggests a serious problem. It is true that in a certain sense the Case III methodology devised by Thurstone, with its σ_k, largely equalizes the $_8O_R$ units actually utilized in any particular quantification. One trouble with the quantifications employed to date is that in our experience the various portions of the learning process are unequally sampled by this procedure (pp. 12 ff.), so that in effect a more or less different unit is used in each study. This means that within any given quantification the unit is approximately constant—namely, the σ_k, though different quantifications are not exactly comparable with one another. As a preliminary suggestion we venture to define the wat, a unit for measuring reaction potential, as follows:

The wat is the mean standard deviation of the momentary reaction potential $(_s\dot{E}_R)$ of standard albino rats, 90 days of age, learning a simple manipulative act requiring a 10-gram pressure by 24-hour distributed trials under 23 hours' hunger, water available, with reward in the form of a 2.5-gram pellet of the usual dry dog food, the mean being taken from all the reinforcement trials producing the habit strength from .75 to .85 habs inclusive.

24. Absolute Zero of Reaction Potential (Z) and the Reaction Threshold ($_sL_R$)

THE CONCEPT of the absolute zero of reaction potential (Z) and that of the reaction threshold ($_sL_R$) are so intimately connected that we find it convenient to treat them in the same section. It is well known that often more than one reinforcement is required before a reaction potential ($_sE_R$) becomes great enough to evoke the reaction (R). This gives rise to the concept of the reaction threshold. To illustrate by use of a case recently studied, it was found that among 59 albino rats trained to perform a simple bar-pressing act, the median animal required approximately two reinforcements before the act was performed as a learned response. This is taken to mean that the absolute zero (Z) of reaction potential ($_sE_R$) was under those conditions lower than the practical threshold ($_sL_R$) by an amount approximately equal to the learning produced by two reinforcements. Since we have an equation representing the course of the learning above the threshold ($_sL_R$) it is a simple matter to insert a negative 2 in the place of N in this equation, and solve for $_sE_R$. This in effect extrapolates the learning curve backward to Z, as follows:

$$_sE_R = 3.084(1 - 10^{-.0305(-2)}) + .04$$
$$= 3.084(1 - 10^{.061}) + .04$$
$$= -.426,$$

which is to say that

$$_sL_R > Z$$

by a reaction potential value of .426. This value and its relationship to the superthreshold portion of the learning curve is illustrated graphically by Figure 6 (p. 30).

Generalizing from the preceding considerations, we arrive at the following postulate (*30*, p. 344):

XIV. A. The reaction threshold ($_sL_R$) stands at an appreciable distance (B) above the absolute zero (Z) of reaction potential ($_sE_R$), i.e.,

$$_sL_R = Z + B. \tag{43}$$

B. No reaction evocation (R) will occur unless the momentary reaction potential at the time exceeds the reaction threshold, i.e., unless

$$_s\dot{\bar{E}}_R > _sL_R.$$

Adding the two reinforcements to those represented by N, we have $\dot{\mathrm{N}}$, and adding the .426 to the reaction potential above the reaction threshold, we have a coefficient of 3.55 in place of the 3.084 of the equation used in the last computation (*13*, p. 513). This gives us an equation for the entire course of learning of

$$_sE_R = 3.55(1 - 10^{-.0305\dot{N}}).$$

This means that the maximum reaction potential (M') attainable in the present situation is 3.55, i.e.,

$$M' = 3.55.$$

Knowing the value of M' and $_8L_R$, it becomes a simple matter to calculate the ratio between the two, which may be useful under certain conditions:

$$\frac{_8L_R}{M'} = \frac{.426}{3.55} = .12. \qquad (44)$$

25. The Competition of Incompatible Reaction Potentials ($_s\bar{E}_R$)

IT WAS POINTED OUT ABOVE that reaction evocation will not take place unless $_s\dot{\bar{E}}_R > {}_sL_R$. It does not follow that under these circumstances R really will take place. The reason is that the stimuli operating at the time may tend to evoke two or more reactions which are impossible of execution simultaneously. For example, the eyelid cannot close and open at the same time; no two words can be spoken at the same time; and so on. It is evident that only the response associated with the greatest reaction potential at the moment ($_s\dot{\bar{E}}_R$) will be evoked. As a matter of fact, this situation is one of the essential conditions which precipitates simple trial-and-error learning.

Generalizing on the above considerations, we arrive at the following corollary (*30*, p. 344):

xii. *When the net reaction potentials* ($_s\bar{E}_R$) *to two or more incompatible reactions* (R) *occur in an organism at the same instant, each in a magnitude greater than* $_sL_R$, *only that reaction whose momentary reaction potential* ($_s\dot{\bar{E}}_R$) *is greatest will be evoked.*

26. Reaction Potential ($_sE_R$) as a Function of Reaction Latency ($_st_R$)

A MAJOR PROTECTION against indeterminacies in a theoretical system which utilizes symbolic constructs or quantitative unobservables is to have the constructs anchored securely (1) to objectively observable and measurable *antecedent* phenomena and conditions, and (2) to observable and measurable *consequent* phenomena and conditions. As already shown, a serious attempt has been made to anchor the constructs represented by $_sH_R$, D, $_sE_R$, $_sI_R$, $\dot{I}_R$, V, K, and J on the antecedent side; the time has now come to consider the problem of anchoring them on the consequent side in an analogous manner. This is a much less laborious task, in part because it is inherently more simple, but also in part because its details are less fully worked out. In the accounts already given of $_sO_R$ and $_sL_R$ we have laid some of the groundwork for the posterior anchoring process.

We recall that when the symbol $_sE_R$ is fully expanded it becomes

$$S \rightarrow s \dashrightarrow E \dashrightarrow r \rightarrow R.$$

From this it is evident that just as S and s are on the antecedent side of the critical symbolic construct, E, so r and R are on the consequent side. But when responses occur they do so in a certain manner which depends upon the magnitude of $_sE_R$. One of the characteristics of response occurrence which offers clues of reaction-

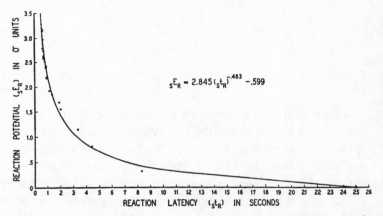

$$_sE_R = 2.845 (_st_R)^{-.483} - .599$$

Figure 24. Graphic representation of reaction potential ($_sE_R$) determined by the paired-comparisons methodology, as a function of median reaction latency ($_st_R$). Reproduced from Gladstone *et al.* (*13*).

potential magnitude on the consequent side is response latency. We accordingly proceed now to the consideration of this relationship.

In this case we are fortunate in having several empirical studies yielding approximations to this function. The first to be published was that by Gladstone *et al.* (*13*, p. 517). The reaction potentials of 25 points throughout 60 reinforcements of 59 albino rats were quantified by the paired-comparisons technique (*39*). These values are represented in Figure 24 as a function of the median latencies. The smooth curve running among the data points was plotted from the equation fitted to the data,

$$_sE_R = 2.845(_st_R)^{-.483} - .599, \tag{45}$$

in which the $-.599$ may here be disregarded as a different determination of a portion of $_sE_R$ below the reaction threshold. This equation presumably represents a fair approximation to the law which we are seeking.

Generalizing on the preceding considerations, we arrive at the following postulate (*30*, p. 344):

XV. Reaction potential ($_sE_R$) is a negatively accelerated decreasing function of the median reaction latency ($_st_R$), i.e.,

$$_sE_R = a_st_R^{-b}.$$

27. Reaction Potential ($_sE_R$) as a Function of Reaction Amplitude (A)

WE CONTINUE THE PROCESS of anchoring our series of symbolic constructs on the consequent side with an attempt to secure a first approximation to an equation representing reaction potential as a function of reaction amplitude (A). The methodology for doing this seems now available, though it has not yet been utilized. This would be to apply the methodology of paired comparisons to the amplitude of the galvanic skin reaction, say, exactly as has been done in the case of reaction latency (*39*). Accordingly we must make the best temporary shift possible until really suitable empirical evidence becomes available, by proceeding in an indirect manner to combine the outcome of two quite different experiments which have been reported.

Hovland (*23*) utilized four groups of 32 human subjects each in setting up the galvanic skin reaction to a tone with 8, 16, 24, and 48 reinforcements respectively. Substituting these Ṅ values in a learning equation obtained from 59 albino rats whose superthreshold reaction potentials had been quantified by means of the paired-comparisons technique based on reaction latencies (*39*), we obtain the corresponding $_sE_R$ values. Figure 25 shows these $_sE_R$ values as a function of the mean amplitude (A) of the galvanic skin reaction. An equation has been

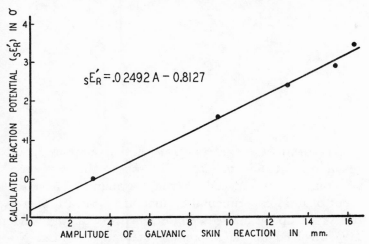

Figure 25. Graphic representation of reaction potential (secured by an indirect determination) as a function of the amplitude (A) of the galvanic skin reaction. Original data published by Hovland (*23*).

fitted to these data, and the straight line running among the data points is plotted from it. This equation is

$$_sE_R' = .02492A - .8127. \qquad (46)$$

Generalizing from the above considerations, we arrive at the following postulate (*30*, p. 344):

XVI. Reaction potential ($_sE_R$) is an increasing linear function of the Tarchanoff galvanic skin reaction amplitude (A), i.e.,

$$_sE_R = cA - b.$$

28. Complete Experimental Extinction (n) as a Function of Reaction Potential ($_sE_R$)

CONTINUING OUR EXAMINATION of the relationship of reaction potential to externally observable response phenomena, we undertake to make a quantitative statement of total experimental extinction (n) as a function of $_sE_R$ set up by massed reinforcements, with the work (W) involved in the response remaining constant. No experimental investigation involving exactly this point has been found. Fortunately there are available two studies which, taken jointly, are functionally related to it; these may serve as a makeshift until more appropriate data become available.

Williams (75) and Perin (56) mass-trained a total of five groups of 40 albino rats each to manipulate a bar requiring 15 grams' pressure to secure a pellet of food reward; the number of reinforcements above the reaction threshold (N) given each group ranged from 5 to 90 (56; 75; 30, p. 106). The median n's were then determined by mass-extinguishing the animals. Now, any actual reaction potential must originate (13) at absolute zero (Z). Assuming that the absolute zero of $_8E_R$ would be two reinforcements more than those recorded by Williams and Perin we add 2 to the Ṇ's to secure the Ṇ's. In order to secure a first approximation to the law

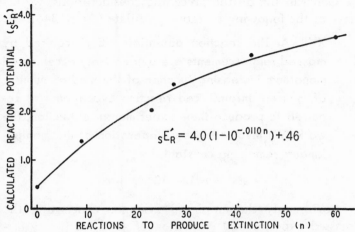

$$_8E'_R = 4.0(1 - 10^{-.0110n}) + .46$$

Figure 26. Graph representing the functional relationship between the number of massed unreinforced reaction evocations (n) required to extinguish a series of calculated reaction potentials ($_8E'_R$) set up by massed reinforcements, the work (W) of operating the manipulandum remaining constant. The smooth line running among the data points represents the fitted equation which states the presumptive law involved. Original data from Williams (75) and Perin (56).

we are seeking we convert these N's into $_8E'_R$'s by substituting them in equation 4 (p. 31), which was derived from separate empirical data cited by Gladstone et al. (13). These presumptive $_8E_R$ values, when each is paired with the corresponding n value, yield the circles shown in Figure 26. An equation fitted to these data is

$$_8E'_R = 4.0(1 - 10^{-.0110n}) + .46. \qquad (47)$$

The smooth curve running among the data points represents this equation which, judging by its proximity to all but one point, is a fair approximation to the presumptive law of $_sE_R = f(n)$ under the stated conditions. Generalizing on the preceding considerations, we arrive at the following tentative postulate (30, p. 344):

XVII. A. The reaction potentials ($_sE_R$) acquired by massed reinforcements are a negatively accelerated monotonic increasing function of the median number of massed unreinforced reaction evocations (n) required to produce their experimental extinction, the work (W) involved in each operation of the manipulandum remaining constant, i.e.,

$$_sE_R = a(1 - 10^{-bn}) + c.$$

Fortunately the empirical evidence concerning the massed experimental extinction of $_sE_R$'s set up by *distributed* trials is somewhat more definite. Yamaguchi (78) trained by different numbers of distributed reinforcements (2, 4, 9, 21) four groups of 34 albino rats each, and a master group of 66, to push a bar for food pellets. The $_sE_R$'s of the several groups were determined for the number of trials used on each group by a paired-comparisons treatment of the response latencies involved, on the master group which received a total of 88 reinforcements. The results of this experiment are shown in Figure 27. An equation fitted to these data is

$$_sE_R = .1225 \times 10^{.0647n} + 2.114. \tag{48}$$

A comparison of Figures 26 and 27 suggests that the massed extinction of reaction potentials set up by massed reinforcements follows a different law from that followed by the massed extinction of those set up by distributed reinforcements. However, see the final note, page 126.

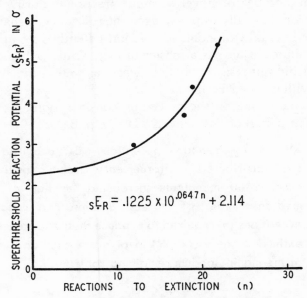

Figure 27. Graph representing the functional relationship between the number of massed unreinforced reaction evocations (n) required to extinguish completely a series of reaction potentials set up by distributed reinforcements. The smooth line running among the data points represents the fitted equation stating the presumptive law involved. Data taken from Yamaguchi (78).

This is not at all surprising in view of the fact that in massed reinforcements the proprioceptive traces of the previous act are present when each act (except the first) occurs and so is involved in the compound stimuli which evoke the R. With distributed reinforcements this is not the case. In the massed experimental extinction of $_sE_R$'s set up by means of massed reinforcement the same thing occurs, which favors resistance. The introduction of a great number of novel stimulus traces (s) during extinction naturally would weaken the resistance in massed experimental extinction of reaction potentials set up by distributed trials. As a matter of fact, Yamaguchi's animals did not resist extinction nearly as well as did those of Williams and Perin.

Generalizing on the preceding considerations, we arrive at part B of Postulate XVII (30, p. 344):

XVII. B. The reaction potentials ($_sE_R$) acquired by quasi-distributed reinforcements are a positively accelerated monotonic increasing function of the median number of massed unreinforced reaction evocations (n) required to produce their experimental extinction, the work (W) involved in each operation of the manipulandum remaining constant, i.e.,

$$_sE_R = a \times 10^{bn} + c.$$

29. Individual Differences

THE PRINCIPLES PRESENTED thus far in this volume
have, on the whole, been considered from the point of
view of their constancy or uniformity as natural molar
laws. We must note here that natural laws are statable
in the form of equations and that such equations contain
values called *constants*, and other values called *variables*.
For example, in the physical equation for falling bodies,

$$s = \tfrac{1}{2}gt^2,$$

g is a constant and t is a variable. This means that if one
wishes to calculate the distance (s) that a body will fall
within a given time (t) at a given point on the earth, the
value of g is taken at the constant value of 32.0992 feet
per second, say, and t may be taken at any of various
values according to the conditions presented by the
problem, such as 1, 3, 10, or 20 seconds. Similarly in
the molar law of habit formation,

$$_sH_R = 1 - 10^{.0305\dot{N}},$$

in the same sense the value .0305 is a constant and $\dot{N}$ is a variable in place of which a value of 2, 5, 20, or 60 reinforcements may be substituted in the calculation of $_sH_R$.

It is important to observe that the "constant" values appearing in the equations expressing natural laws are not necessarily constant. For example, the g appearing in the law of falling bodies varies quite perceptibly at different geographical positions. Similarly, but much more markedly, the "constants" appearing in the laws of molar behavior are not constant. Presumably if a group of organisms strictly comparable in all other respects to those from which this equation was secured were tested on the same behavior form, a value within the sampling range of .0305 would be again secured. But if older or younger or diseased organisms were used, or if a different genetic strain or a different species, and particularly if single individuals were used, presumably rather different exponential values would result.

In view of these and related considerations, the hypothesis is here being put forward that both individual differences and species differences appear in natural molar behavior laws as variable values of the "constants" involved. Unfortunately the methodology of securing equations from quantified behavioral data has been developed so recently and is so complicated by behavioral oscillation that little evidence on individual differences is available. A single study of this type was begun by H. Richmond Davis, but it has not yet been completed. A sizable segment of behavioral science accordingly remains practically untouched—one quite different from that investigated by factor analysis. We believe that the latter goes much deeper than do ordinary molar principles, cutting across them sharply. Quite possibly it even involves such things as basic physiological determiners.

Generalizing on the preceding considerations, we arrive at our last postulate to date (*32*):

XVIII. The "constant" numerical values appearing in equations representing primary molar behavioral laws vary from species to species, from individual to individual, and from some physiological states to others in the same individual at different times, all quite apart from the factor of behavioral oscillation ($_sO_R$).

Notes

THE HISTORY OF THE PRESENT SET OF POSTULATES

The matter of isolating and formulating a set of quantitative postulates or mathematical primary principles upon which may be based a true natural science designed to mediate the deduction of a system as complex as that of mammalian behavior is a formidable undertaking. It is quite simple to write out the blank forms of equations such as $x = f(y)$, but it often requires careful planning, great labor, and a certain amount of skill to determine what the function actually is and to check it empirically, determining at the same time the value of the numerical constants. All this takes much time and effort. The detailed history of such a process would itself require a fair-sized volume.

Very briefly, the procedure typically begins with selecting two or three principles, often isolated by earlier workers, from the complex of data involving a certain class of experiments, generalizing and quantifying them as equations, and attempting to apply them quantitatively to a wider range of phenomena. When it would seem that a combination of principles ought to mediate the deduction of an empirically known phenomenon but clearly does not do so, the principles in question are reëxamined for the possible revision of one or more of them to the end that they will yield the deduction of the phenomenon in question and still mediate the true deductions already to the credit of the critical postulates.

Sometimes the deduction failure may appear to be the result of ignoring some law not yet formulated. In such a case an empirical situation is sought for, where all the factors are held constant except the one in question; the function is plotted and an equation is fitted to the empirical curve; the equation is then tried out deductively in more general situations with other principles which presumably are also operating with it. Thus a large element of trial and error is involved in the process, with failures relatively more frequent among the early trials than among the later ones.

The most detailed record of these trials by the present writer may be found scattered through twenty-five volumes of handwritten notebooks. These began in October, 1915, and extend to the present time. The system grew very slowly. As it took on more definite form the author began to present from time to time somewhat formalized statements regarding it to his seminar groups. These statements were made in the form of mimeographed memoranda. Three volumes of these memoranda were assembled, substantially bound, and copies were deposited in the Yale University Library and in the libraries of two or three other universities where a certain amount of interest was manifested in such matters. The bound memoranda extend over the academic years 1936–1938, 1939–1940, and 1940–1944 (*37; 29; 31*).

From time to time during these three periods the principles which seemed most promising at the moment were gathered together in a numbered series, sometimes accompanied by a few deductions based on the postulates. The dates of the chief of these series follow, with the pages of the volume where found:

On September 4, 1936, the writer used a much abbreviated version of an earlier set of postulates as the basis of an address given by him as retiring president of the American Psychological Association. This was published in routine form (*26*) in January, 1937. The next published version of this system appeared in the jointly prepared volume, *Mathematico-deductive Theory of Rote Learning* (*38*). The most recently preceding published form is presented in the bold-faced type sections scattered through the volume, *Principles of Behavior* (*30*).

$_8E_R$ AS A FUNCTION OF THE DELAY IN REINFORCEMENT

There is some reason to believe that the law of the delay in reinforcement (J) may not prove to be exactly as formulated in the text. At bottom, this uncertainty like somewhat similar ones in connection with D, V, and K, may lie in the fact that the material analyzed needed to be designated as $_8E_R'$, rather than as $_8E_R$. One special reason for the uncertainty in regard to J, the correlation of the exponents in the equations with the amount of delay, is mentioned in the text.

A second reason, which may be related to the first, is that if the gross empirical exponents of the curves were to be taken as the basis for the plotting of Figure 14, the fitted relationship would yield the equation:

$$_8E'_R = 1.19 \times 10^{-.223T} - .078(T + 2.30),$$

which is of the same form as that found by Perin (*57*, p. 46). Actually the fact that animals trained by the various techniques employed sooner or later find a delay under which they do not learn at all shows that the J function really passes into a negative value with sufficiently large values of T. Our equation fitted to the data shown in Figure 14 does not do this, though Perin's equation and the one given above really do so.

AN EARLIER ACCOUNT OF THE CONSTITUTION OF REACTION POTENTIAL

The original published account of the constitution of reaction potential (*30*, p. 178, equation 16) was not clear owing partly to the expository difficulty of treating $_8E_R$, as distinguished from $_8H_R$, before the principle of primary motivation had been presented. In current symbolism, the $_8H_R$ of the original equation, #16, should be changed to $_8E_R$, and the M, to D. The present account agrees in the general multiplicative relationship assumed at that time. It has one new factor (V) and omits one factor, that of the temporal asynchronism of the conditioned to the unconditioned stimulus in conditioned-reaction formation (*41*).

HISTORY OF THE HYPOTHESIS REGARDING HABIT STRENGTH SUMMATION (+)

This hypothesis was first put forward in 1939 with a deductive presentation in substantially its present form (but in different notation) worked out by P. T. Perkins (*27*, pp. 20, 21) for the summation of two habit strengths. In 1943 the Perkins equation was again presented (*30*, p. 223) and a second, more general, formula deduced by A. S. Day and capable of yielding a parallel summation for any number of habit strengths at the same time was also published (*30*, p. 200) and utilized in a further deduction (*30*, p. 195). At the same time there was published a long terminal note (*30*, pp. 223–224) on "the difficulty of applying the habit-summation equations in quantitative detail to concrete behavior situations." It was held that despite these difficulties a number of quasi-quantitative but empirically testable theorems could be derived from the equations even under the conditions then obtaining, three such theorems being specified.

In 1945, P. E. Meehl published (*47*) an excellent critical examination of the possible utility of the Perkins-Day formulae. In this he pointed out that there were involved in the Perkins-Day derivations the assumptions (a) that the rate of growth of the $_sH_R$'s to be combined must be the same, (b) that the asymptote or ultimate limit of this growth of all $_sH_R$'s involved must be the same, and (c) that the two assumptions involved in such summation are rarely or never exactly encountered in the situation under his special consideration at the time (afferent interaction).

Fortunately the dilemma posed by Meehl's critique is now clarified in part. The evidence has become fairly clear that assumption (b) is true, i.e., that the asymptotes of all habit-strength growth functions alike are 1.00 (p. 32). On the other hand, the evidence regarding assumption (a) is very complex and the conclusion is far from clear regarding the *rate* of growth. The fact appears to be that responses are never caused by $_sH_R$ alone or by V or J or K or D alone, but by all these factors making up $_sE_R$ acting jointly (p. 59). As indicated on the preceding pages, it requires a fairly complicated procedure to isolate $_sH_R$ as such. Even the hypothetical separation of two stimulus elements from a habit based on a simultaneous stimulus compound, such as that instanced above (p. 60), would result merely in a divided reaction potential. And if the intensities of the two stimulus components were unequal the $_sE_R$'s would be different because of different V's, even if the $_sH_R$'s were identical.

But the procedure for determining the rate of habit growth is quite clear even if the conclusion is not. An equal rate of growth would be shown by an equality of the exponents in the $_sH_R$ equations when, and if, secured, and a different rate of growth would be indicated by a systematic difference in the exponents correlated with the varying conditions under which the habit was acquired, e.g., such as the delay in reinforcement (Figure 13, p. 54). Indeed, it may very well turn out that delay in reinforcement will have a systematic variation in habit growth rate, and the others will have an equal rate. We must reserve judgment until adequate evidence becomes available. Rather elaborate plans were made (*34*, p. 24 ff.) to test out empirically the soundness of the Perkins-Day formulae, but they were abandoned because time and energy for carrying out the experiments were lacking.

INITIAL RISE IN $_s\bar{E}_R$ DURING EXPERIMENTAL EXTINCTION

It has repeatedly been observed that under certain conditions the $_s\bar{E}_R$ early in experimental extinction rises instead of falls (*25*, pp. 438–439). This rise does not appear in Figure 2 of the study by Wilcoxon *et al.* (*74*), p. 79 above. The reason is not clear.

ADVERSE CRITICISMS OF AFFERENT STIMULUS INTERACTION

This hypothesis has been more severely criticized than any other of the present set of primary principles (*46*, pp. 25–26; *62*, pp. 642–643; *65*, p. 279). It has been objected, for example, that the postulate lacks proof. This is quite true. A postulate is an hypothesis and it is perfectly orthodox scientific methodology for hypotheses to originate without complete proof; when, and if, adequate proof is supplied the proposition ceases to be an hypothesis and becomes a true law in a scientific theory. An ambitious experimental program (*34*, pp. 27 ff.) comparable to that of quantifying $_sE_R$ (*12; 39; 13; 79*) was recently formulated (1945) to secure definitive evidence but lack of time and energy forced its abandonment.

A very different objection to afferent stimulus interaction is that the principle is neurological and that to place a neurological principle in a molar system commits some kind of fallacy (*19*, p. 112). No doubt this misunderstanding arose mainly from the fact that the principle was first called "afferent neural interaction," an expository clumsiness misleading to many readers. The reply to the fallacy objection is that this principle is at bottom purely molar, like $_sH_R$ and $_sE_R$, which are neural in the same sense. This is clearly shown on p. 94 by the methodology put forward for quantifying afferent stimulus interaction. In view of the use designed to be made of equation 41 above (*33*, p. 139), Hilgard's assertion that our treatment of the problem "buries it in the nervous system" (*19*, p. 82) seems about as contrary to the logic of the actual hypothesis as could well be imagined.

BEHAVIORAL OSCILLATION AS REACTION POTENTIAL ($_sE_R$) CROSSES THE REACTION THRESHOLD ($_sL_R$) DURING LEARNING

It has been pointed out above (p. 99) that $_sO_R$ probably begins with a zero dispersion when $_sE_R$ stands at zero and increases as a growth function, at least through the first eight or nine reinforcements. This is very different from the hypothesis earlier utilized (*38*, p. 78; *30*, pp. 314, 319) which was that the dispersion of $_sO_R$ is invariable, i.e., the same at the beginning of the acquisition of $_sE_R$ as at its maximum.

This changed assumption naturally greatly reduces the amount of variability in the probability (p) of reaction evocation in simple reaction situations as the threshold is being crossed by $_sE_R$ during the learning process. Felsinger's empirical results indicate that in his experiment once the response had risen above the reaction threshold and had been reinforced, it relatively infrequently failed to do so during the continuing learning process, which is what would be expected by the present revised hypothesis regarding $_sO_R$ dispersions. This contrasts sharply with the former interpretations of the very slow increases in p observed in the case of conditioned blinking (30, p. 332) and in rote learning (30, p. 307). It is now believed that these latter forms of learning are in reality cases of simple trial-and-error learning, and that what was formerly supposed to be the reaction threshold was a strong competing reaction (R') either already in existence before the learning in question was begun, or one which was being acquired at the same time.

The first type of R' presumably is found in the case of the conditioned wink, say in the case of the Hilgard-Marquis dog (30, p. 332). The open eye is a necessary part of the receptor-exposure act ordinarily mediating adaptive behavior throughout life, and so presumably is much reinforced and therefore has a very strong behavior tendency ($_sE_R$). The second type of behavioral competition is seen in the numerous remote associative tendencies based on stimulus traces in rote learning (38) and in serial compound trial-and-error learning (3; 68). In the learning of paired associates, even with continually changing orders of presentations, the competing R's could be attached to the stimuli of the experimental situation which continue largely unchanged throughout the learning process.

REACTION POTENTIAL ($_sE_R$) AS A FUNCTION OF A AND n

In 1943 (30, pp. 337 ff.), we postulated that *both* n and A were linear functions of $_sE_R$, largely because both were approximately growth functions of N. So far that conjecture seems to have been confirmed by subsequent evidence in regard to A (see Figure 25). It very definitely is not confirmed in regard to n (see Figures 26 and 27). As a matter of fact, the indirect procedure used in the determinations of all these figures might lead to any of these forms as artifacts because of the variability in the constants operating in the two groups of subjects used in the indirect determinations. This means that Figures 25, 26, and 27, together with the associated postulates, must still be regarded as very tentative, useful chiefly in calling attention to the problems. Fortunately these problems are now capable of a fairly direct experimental solution.

Glossary of Symbols

A = amplitude; a constant.

a = empirical constant.

B = exponential constant.

b = empirical constant.

β_2 = constant involving leptokurtic distribution.

$C = {}_sH_R + {}_sH_R'$.

C_D = condition producing a drive.

c = empirical constant.

D = effective or gross drive; $D = D' \times \epsilon$.

D' = drive proper.

d = the difference between two stimuli.

${}_sE_R$ = reaction potential.

${}_sE_R'$ = various approximations to ${}_sE_R$; some other ${}_sE_R$.

${}_s\underline{E}_R$ = reaction potential resulting from stimulus generalization.

${}_s\dot{E}_R$ = the portion of ${}_sE_R$ lying above the reaction threshold.

${}_s\bar{E}_R$ = effective reaction potential; ${}_sE_R \doteq \dot{I}_R$.

${}_s\dot{\bar{E}}_R$ = momentary reaction potential.

e = mathematical constant, sometimes taken as 10.

f = function of ( ).

${}_sH_R$ = habit; habit strength.

${}_sH_R'$ = some other habit strength.

$_8\dot{H}_R = {}_8H_R \times V_1.$

$_8\bar{H}_R$ = habit strength resulting from stimulus generalization.

h = hours of food deprivation.

I_R = reaction inhibition.

I'_R = reaction inhibition remaining after a period of spontaneous recovery.

$\dot{I}_R = I_R + {}_8I_R.$

$\dot{\underset{.}{I}}_R = {}_8\underset{.}{E}_R$; enough $\dot{I}_R$ to neutralize the superthreshold reaction potential.

$_8I_R$ = conditioned inhibition.

$_8\underline{I}_R$ = generalized inhibitory potential.

J = component of reaction potential; $J = 10^{-jt}$ where t is the delay in reinforcement in seconds.

j = an empirical exponential constant.

j.n.d. = just noticeable difference; discrimination threshold.

K = component of reaction potential; incentive motivation.

K_a = water incentive.

K_f = food incentive; $K_f = 1 - 10^{-a\sqrt{w}}.$

$_8L_R$ = minimum reaction potential evoking reaction; reaction threshold.

log = logarithm.

M = the learning maximum; this is 100 habs in terms of $_8H_R.$

N = number of reinforcements in general.

$\dot{N}$ = number of reinforcements from beginning of learning, i.e., from absolute zero (Z).

$\underset{.}{N}$ = number of superthreshold reinforcements.

n = number of unreinforced reaction evocations required to produce experimental extinction.

$\dot{n}$ = ordinal number of unreinforced reaction evocations at a given time.

$_8O_R$ = momentary behavioral oscillation.

R = response; an act of some kind.

S = stimulus; stimulus energy.

$\dot{S}$ = a stimulus in the process of being conditioned.

S' = theoretical stimulus intensity which is functionally equivalent to a given molar afferent impulse.

$\dot{S}'$ = theoretical recruitment phase of molar afferent energy impulse.

$\underset{.}{S}'$ = theoretical subsident phase of molar afferent energy impulse.

S_D = drive stimulus.

s = neurophysiological afferent impulse evoked by S.

s_D = drive receptor afferent impulse.

$\breve{s}$ = afferent impulse as modified by afferent interaction.

s' = theoretical molar afferent impulse corresponding to s; molar stimulus trace intensity; $s' = \log S'$.

$\dot{s}'$ = theoretical recruitment phase of molar afferent impulse.

$\underset{.}{s}'$ = theoretical subsident phase of molar afferent impulse.

t = time (usually in seconds); duration; delay in reinforcement.

$\underset{.}{t}$ = time since the termination (or beginning) of a stimulation.

t' = time since the maximum of the recruitment phase of a stimulus trace; $t' = \underset{.}{t} - .450''$.

$_s t_R$ = reaction latency; reaction time.

$_s U_R$ = unlearned receptor-effector connection.

V = stimulus-intensity dynamism; $V = 1 - 10^{-a \log S}$.

V_1 = stimulus-intensity dynamism involved in original learning.

V_2 = stimulus-intensity dynamism which evokes a response.

W = work involved in a response (R).

w = weight of food incentive.

y = distribution of momentary behavioral oscillation ($_s O_R$).

Z = absolute zero of reaction potential.

Δ = increment.

ϵ = inanition component of food privation drive; $\epsilon = \dfrac{D}{D'}$.

σ = the standard deviation.

$\dot{+}$ = behavioral summation.

$\doteq$ = behavioral withdrawal.

$\dashrightarrow$ = acquired receptor-effector connection.

$\rightarrow$ = unlearned connection.

$\rightsquigarrow$ = causal relationship other than receptor-effector connection.

References

1. ANDERSON, E. E. The externalization of drive. I. Theoretical considerations. *Psychol. Rev.*, 1941, *48*, 204–224.
2. ANDERSON, E. E. The externalization of drive. III. Maze learning by non-rewarded and by satiated rats. *J. Genet. Psychol.*, 1941, *59*, 397–426.
3. ARNOLD, W. J. Simple reaction chains and their integration. I. Homogeneous chaining with terminal reinforcement. *J. Comp. and Physiol. Psychol.*, 1947, *40*, 349–363.
4. BROWN, J. S. The generalization of approach responses as a function of stimulus intensity and strength of motivation. *J. Comp. Psychol.*, 1942, *33*, 209–226.
5. BUGELSKI, R. Extinction with and without sub-goal reinforcement. *J. Comp. Psychol.*, 1938, *26*, 121–133.
6. CATTELL, J. McK. The influence of the intensity of the stimulus on the length of the reaction time. *Brain*, 1886, *8*, 512–515.
7. COWLES, J. T. Food-tokens as incentives for learning by chimpanzees. *Comp. Psychol. Monogr.*, 1937, *14*, No. 5.
8. CRESPI, L. P. Quantitative variation of incentive and performance in the white rat. *Amer. J. Psychol.*, 1942, *55*, 467–517.

9. CRESPI, L. P. Amount of reinforcement and level of performance. *Psychol. Rev.*, 1944, *51*, 341–357.

10. ELLSON, D. G. Quantitative studies of the interaction of simple habits. I. Recovery from specific and generalized effects of extinction. *J. Exper. Psychol.*, 1938, *23*, 339–358.

11. FELSINGER, J. M. The effect of an induced oestrous as an irrelevant drive on the learning of a maze habit, and on its persistence during satiation. Ph. D. thesis, on file Yale Univ. Library, 1948.

12. FELSINGER, J. M., GLADSTONE, A. I., YAMAGUCHI, H. G., and HULL, C. L. Reaction latency ($_{s}t_{R}$) as a function of the number of reinforcements (N). *J. Exper. Psychol.*, 1947, *37*, 214–228.

13. GLADSTONE, A. I., YAMAGUCHI, H. G., HULL, C. L., and FELSINGER, J. M. Some functional relationships of reaction potential ($_{s}E_{R}$) and related phenomena. *J. Exper. Psychol.*, 1947, *37*, 510–526.

14. GRAHAM, C. H. Vision: III. Some neural correlations. Chapter 15 in *Handbook of General Experimental Psychology*, Carl Murchison, editor. Worcester, Mass.: Clark Univ. Press, 1934.

15. GRICE, G. R. The relation of secondary reinforcement to delayed reward in visual discrimination learning. *J. Exper. Psychol.*, 1948, *38*, 1–16.

16. GRINDLEY, G. C. Experiments on the influence of the amount of reward on learning in young chickens. *Brit. J. Psychol.*, 1929, *20*, 173–180.

17. GUILFORD, J. P. *Psychometric Methods*. New York: McGraw-Hill Book Co., 1936.

18. HECHT, S. Vision: II. The nature of the photoreceptor process. Chapter 14 in *Handbook of General Experimental Psychology*, Carl Murchison, editor. Worcester, Mass.: Clark Univ. Press, 1934.

19. HILGARD, E. R. *Theories of Learning*. New York: Appleton-Century-Crofts, Inc., 1948.

20. HOUSEHOLDER, A. S., and LANDAHL, H. D. Mathematical biophysics of the central nervous system. *Mathematical Biophysics Monog. Series*. No. 1. Bloomington, Ind.: The Principia Press, Inc., 1945.

21. HOVLAND, C. I. The generalization of conditioned responses. I. The sensory generalization of conditioned responses with varying frequencies of tone. *J. Gen. Psychol.*, 1937, *17*, 125–148.

22. HOVLAND, C. I. The generalization of conditioned responses: II. The sensory generalization of conditioned responses with varying intensities of tone. *J. Genet. Psychol.*, 1937, *51*, 279–291.

23. HOVLAND, C. I. The generalization of conditioned responses: IV. The effects of varying amounts of reinforcement upon the degree of generalization of conditioned responses. *J Exper. Psychol.*, 1937, *21*, 261–276.

24. HULL, C. L. The goal gradient hypothesis and maze learning. *Psychol. Rev.*, 1932, *39*, 25–43.

25. HULL, C. L. Learning: II. The factor of the conditioned reflex. Chapter 9 in *Handbook of General Experimental Psychology*, Carl Murchison, editor. Worcester, Mass.: Clark Univ. Press, 1934.

26. HULL, C. L. Mind, mechanism, and adaptive behavior. *Psychol. Rev.*, 1937, *44*, 1–32.

27. HULL, C. L. The problem of stimulus equivalence in behavior theory. *Psychol. Rev.*, 1939, *46*, 9–30.

28. HULL, C. L. Simple trial-and-error learning—an empirical investigation. *J. Comp. Psychol.*, 1939, *27*, 233–258.

29. HULL, C. L. Psychological Seminar Memoranda, 1939–1940. Bound mimeographed manuscript on file in the libraries of Yale Univ., Univ. of Iowa, and Oberlin College.

30. HULL, C. L. *Principles of Behavior*. New York: D. Appleton-Century Co., Inc., 1943.

31. HULL, C. L. Psychological Memoranda, 1940–1944. Bound mimeographed manuscript on file in the libraries of Yale Univ., Univ. of Iowa, and Univ. of North Carolina.

32. HULL, C. L. The place of innate individual and species differences in a natural-science theory of behavior. *Psychol. Rev.*, 1945, *52*, 55–60.

33. HULL, C. L. The discrimination of stimulus configurations and the hypothesis of afferent neural interaction. *Psychol. Rev.*, 1945, *52*, 133–142.

34. HULL, C. L. Research Memorandum. (Concerning the empirical determination of the form of certain basic molar behavioral equations and the values of their associated constants.) 1946. Bound manuscript on file in the libraries of Yale Univ., Univ. of Iowa, Univ. of North Carolina, and Oberlin College.

35. HULL, C. L. The problem of primary stimulus generalization. *Psychol. Rev.*, 1947, *54*, 120–134.

36. HULL, C. L. Stimulus intensity dynamism (V) and stimulus generalization. *Psychol. Rev.*, 1949, *56*, 67–76.

37. HULL, C. L., and MOWRER, O. H. Hull's Psychological Seminars, 1936–1938. Bound mimeographed manuscript on file in the libraries of Yale Univ., Univ. Chicago, and Univ. of North Carolina.

38. HULL, C. L., HOVLAND, C. I., ROSS, R. T., HALL, M., PERKINS, D. T., and FITCH, F. B. *Mathematico-deductive Theory of Rote Learning*. New Haven: Yale Univ. Press, 1940.

39. HULL, C. L., FELSINGER, J. M., GLADSTONE, A. I., and YAMAGUCHI, H. G. A proposed quantification of habit strength. *Psychol. Rev.*, 1947, *54*, 237–254.

40. KENDLER, H. H. The influence of simultaneous hunger and thirst drives upon the learning of two opposed

spatial responses of the white rat. *J. Exper. Psychol.*, 1946, *36*, 212–220.

41. KIMBLE, G. A. Conditioning as a function of the time between conditioned and unconditioned stimuli. *J. Exper. Psychol.*, 1947, *37*, 1–15.

42. KIMBLE, G. A. An experimental test of a two-factor theory of inhibition. *J. Exper. Psychol.*, 1949, *39*, 15–23.

43. KOCH, S., and DANIEL, W. J. The effect of satiation on the behavior mediated by a habit of maximum strength. *J. Exper. Psychol.*, 1945, *35*, 167–187.

44. KÖHLER, W., *Gestalt Psychology.* New York: Liveright Pub. Co., 1929.

45. KÖHLER, W., *Dynamics in Psychology.* New York: Liveright Pub. Co., 1940.

46. LEEPER, R. Dr. Hull's Principles of Behavior. *J. Genet. Psychol.*, 1944, *65*, 3–52.

47. MEEHL, P. E. An examination of the treatment of stimulus patterning in Professor Hull's *Principles of Behavior. Psychol. Rev.*, 1945, *52*, 324–332.

48. MILLER, N. E. Studies of fear as an acquirable drive: I. Fear as motivation and fear-reduction as reinforcement in the learning of new responses. *J. Exper. Psychol.*, 1948, *38*, 89–101.

49. MILLER, N. E. Learnable drives and rewards. Chapter 13 in *Handbook of Experimental Psychology*, S. S. Stevens editor. New York: John Wiley and Sons, 1951.

50. MILLER, N. E., and DOLLARD, J. *Social Learning and Imitation.* New Haven: Yale Univ. Press, 1941.

51. MOWRER, O. H. A stimulus response analysis of anxiety and its role as a reinforcing agent. *Psychol. Rev.*, 1939, *46*, 553–565.

52. MOWRER, O. H., and JONES, H. M. Extinction and behavior variability as functions of effortfulness of task. *J. Exper. Psychol.*, 1943, *33*, 369–386.

53. PASSEY, G. E. The influence of intensity of unconditioned

stimulus upon acquisition of a conditioned response. *J. Exper. Psychol.*, 1948, *38*, 420–428.

54. PAVLOV, I. P. *Conditioned Reflexes.* (Trans. by G. V. Anrep.) London: Oxford Univ. Press, 1927.

55. PEARSON, K. *Tables for Statisticians and Biometricians*, Part I. (3rd ed.). Cambridge, England: Cambridge Univ. Press, 1930.

56. PERIN, C. T. Behavior potentiality as a joint function of the amount of training and the degree of hunger at the time of extinction. *J. Exper. Psychol.*, 1942, *30*, 93–113.

57. PERIN, C. T. A quantitative investigation of the delay-of-reinforcement gradient. *J. Exper. Psychol.*, 1943, *32*, 37–51.

58. PERKINS, C. C. The relation of secondary reward to gradients of reinforcement. Ph.D. thesis, University of Iowa, 1946.

59. PIÉRON, H. Nouvelles recherches sur l'analyse du temps de latence sensorielle et sur la loi qui relie le temps à l'intensité d'excitation. *L'Année psychologique*, 1920, *22*, 58–142.

60. RASHEVSKY, N. *Advances and applications of mathematical biology.* Chicago: Univ. of Chicago Press, 1940.

61. REYNOLDS, B. The acquisition of a trace conditioned response as a function of the magnitude of the stimulus trace. *J. Exper. Psychol.*, 1945, *35*, 15–30.

62. RITCHIE, B. F. Hull's treatment of learning. *Psychol. Bull.*, 1944, *41*, 640–652.

63. SALTZMAN, I., and KOCH, S. The effect of low intensities of hunger on the behavior mediated by a habit of maximum strength. *J. Exper. Psychol.*, 1948, *38*, 347–370.

64. SKINNER, B. F. *The behavior of organisms*, New York: D. Appleton-Century Co., Inc., 1938.

65. SKINNER, B. F. Principles of behavior, by Clark L. Hull. *Amer. J. Psychol.*, 1944, *57*, 276–281.

66. SPENCE, K. W. The role of secondary reinforcement in delayed reward learning. *Psychol. Rev.*, 1947, *54*, 1–8.

67. SPENCE, K. W. Theoretical interpretations of learning.
Chapter 18 in *Handbook of experimental psychology*, S. S.
Stevens, editor. New York: John Wiley and Sons,
1951.

68. SPROW, A. S. Reactively homogeneous compound trial-
and-error learning with distributed trials and terminal
reinforcement. *J. Exper. Psychol.*, 1947, *37*, 197–213.

69. THURSTONE, L. L. A law of comparative judgment. *Psychol.
Rev.*, 1927, *34*, 273–286.

70. THURSTONE, L. L. Psychophysical analysis. *Amer. J.
Psychol.*, 1927, *38*, 368–389.

71. THURSTONE, L. L. Stimulus dispersion in the method of
constant stimuli. *J. Exper. Psychol.*, 1932, *15*, 284–289.

72. WARDEN, C. J., JENKINS, T. N., and WARNER, L. H.
Introduction to comparative psychology. New York: Ronald
Press, 1934.

73. WEBB, W. B. The motivational aspect of an irrelevant
drive in the behavior of the white rat. *J. Exper. Psychol.*,
1949, *39*, 1–14.

74. WILCOXON, H. C., HAYS, R., and HULL, C. L. A preliminary determination of the functional relationship of
effective reaction potential ($_s\bar{E}_R$) and the ordinal number of Vincentized extinction reactions (ṅ). *J. Exper.
Psychol.*, 1950, *40*, 194–199.

75. WILLIAMS, S. B. Resistance to extinction as a function of
the number of reinforcements. *J. Exper. Psychol.*, 1938,
23, 506–521.

76. WOLFLE, H. M. Time factors in conditioning finger-with-
drawal. *J. Gen. Psychol.*, 1930, *4*, 372–379.

77. WOLFLE, H. M. Conditioning as a function of the inter-
val between the conditioned and the original stimulus.
J. Gen. Psychol., 1932, *7*, 80–103.

78. YAMAGUCHI, H. G. Quantification of motivation. Ph.D. thesis, Yale Univ., 1949.

79. YAMAGUCHI, H. G., HULL, C. L., FELSINGER, J. M., and GLADSTONE, A. I. Characteristics of dispersions based on the pooled momentary reaction potentials ($_8\dot{\bar{E}}_R$) of a group. *Psychol. Rev.*, 1948, *55*, 216–238.

Index of Subjects

Act learning. *See* Learning.

Afferent neural impulse, 5–11.

Afferent stimulus interaction, 6, 93–95, 124–125.

Amplitude of reaction, and reaction potential, 108–109, 126–127.

Anticipatory goal reaction, 24.

Anticipatory relaxation, 27.

Asynchronism, of the oscillations of reaction potential, 99.

Behavior, individual, 1–2; innate, 3–4, 12, 15 f., 33; mammalian, 2; molar, 29; molar theory of, 5–6; primary laws of mammalian, 1; theory versus neurophysiology, 5–6.

Behavioral summation, of habit strengths, 60–63, 122–124; of incentive substances, 70–72; of reaction potentials, 64–65.

Behavioral withdrawal, in terms of habit strength, 66–67; in terms of reaction potential, 68–69.

Conditioned inhibition, 27, 73 f.

Conditioned-reflex learning, 7–11, 15–20.

Conditioning, experimental, 7–11, 15–20.

Construct, quantitative theoretical, 12–14; symbolic, 6, 29, 105.

Delay in reinforcement, 52 f., 121–122.

Drive, and drive reduction, 15 f., 27; and the reaction threshold, 36–38; as a function of drive conditions, 35–39; as secondary motivation, 21–25; electric shock as a, 26 f.; externalization of, 21 f.; fear as a, 21–27; generalization of, 39–40; generalization to hunger drive from thirst, 39–40; habit strength acting jointly with primary, 33–39; in conditioning, 18–20; in relation to unlearned behavior, 3–4; in trial-and-error learning, 16–19; inhibitory potential as a negative, 73 f.; proper, 36–39; quantification of the hunger, 34–39; secondary, 21–25, 28; secondary motivation and primary, 21–25; sex, 22–23, 40.

Drive condition, and secondary motivation, 21–25; examples of, 15–18.

Drive state, 15.

Books, in print, published by the Yale University Press
for the Institute of Human Relations

THE CRAVING FOR SUPERIORITY. *By Raymond Dodge and Eugen Kahn*

THE VITAMIN B REQUIREMENT OF MAN. *By George R. Cowgill*

UNION-MANAGEMENT COOPERATION IN THE "STRETCH-OUT." *By R. Carter Nyman and Elliot Dunlap Smith*

A HANDBOOK OF SOCIAL STATISTICS OF NEW HAVEN, CONNECTICUT. *By Thelma Dreis*

NEW LIGHT ON DELINQUENCY AND ITS TREATMENT. *By William Healy and Augusta Bronner*

FRUSTRATION AND AGGRESSION. *By John Dollard and others*

CITIZENS WITHOUT WORK. *By E. Wight Bakke*

MATHEMATICO-DEDUCTIVE THEORY OF ROTE LEARNING. *By Clark L. Hull and others*

NEW HAVEN NEGROES. *By Robert Austin Warner*

SMOKE FROM THEIR FIRES. *By Clellan S. Ford.*

SOCIAL LEARNING AND IMITATION. *By Neal E. Miller and John Dollard*

BECOMING A KWOMA. *By John W. M. Whiting.*

ITALIAN OR AMERICAN? *By Irvin L. Child*

A SOCIAL PSYCHOLOGY OF WAR AND PEACE. *By Mark A. May*

DATE DUE
